LEAD
LIKE A PRO

www.mascotbooks.com

Lead Like A Pro: Effective Leadership Styles for Athletic Coaches

©2021 Dr. Matthew Raidbard. All Rights Reserved. No part of this publication may be reproduced, stored in a retrieval system or transmitted in any form by any means electronic, mechanical, or photocopying, recording or otherwise without the permission of the author.

For more information, please contact:
Mascot Books
620 Herndon Parkway #320
Herndon, VA 20170
info@mascotbooks.com

CPSIA Code: PRV0621A
Library of Congress Control Number: 2021901445
ISBN-13: 978-1-64543-410-8

Printed in the United States

*For my wife, Lindsay—I could never
have accomplished something like writing
this book without your love and support.*

*For Emma and Madeline—everything
I do in life is for you.*

LEAD

LIKE A PRO

EFFECTIVE LEADERSHIP STYLES
FOR ATHLETIC COACHES

Dr. Matthew Raidbard

TABLE OF CONTENTS

INTRODUCTION:
COACHES ARE LEADERS...1

CHAPTER I:
DON'T HAVE A LEADERSHIP IDENTITY CRISIS......................... 9

CHAPTER II:
COACHES ARE LIKE SNOWFLAKES..23

CHAPTER III:
PERCEIVED VS. ACTUAL LEADERSHIP STYLE 35

CHAPTER IV:
I THINK, THEREFORE I MUST BE..41

CHAPTER V:
WHO AM I? 55

CHAPTER VI:
LET'S GET ANALYTICAL... 73

CHAPTER VII:
TRANSCENDING BEYOND THE ROLE OF "COACH"............... 79

CHAPTER VIII:
WHAT DOES SUCCESS LOOK LIKE?.. 87

CHAPTER IX:
FINAL REFLECTIONS ON LEADERSHIP....................................... 93

CITATIONS 103

INTRODUCTION

COACHES ARE LEADERS

Today, athletic coaches are asked to wear many hats. At various times, coaches are asked to be teachers, role models, mentors, therapists, travel agents, mediators, advisors, and a whole host of other important roles that are never in the job description. When I first broke in as a men's college basketball coach, I honestly thought most of my job, and corresponding responsibilities, was going to take place on the basketball court. I was twenty-two years old and had no idea what I was walking into, let alone the breadth of roles I was going to play aside from instructing my athletes on the court and putting together winning game plans. Within weeks of starting, my perception of what a college basketball coach did on a daily basis was turned upside down.

In one of the first meetings I had with my head coach, he laid out numerous leadership lessons. Several of those lessons made an impression. Even though I did not fully understand that his advice, and more advice I would receive from different coaches early in my career, would have an impact on my leadership practice moving forward, the seeds were planted nonetheless. The lessons

I remember were not ground-breaking bits of wisdom that were going to instantly transform me from a wide-eyed college graduate starting out in the business into John Wooden, but when it comes to leadership, even simple and succinct lessons can have a big impact.

"Don't ever let the athletes wait for you." When my first head coach gave me that bit of advice, I'll admit, I did not completely understand why this directive was important. Years later, I would realize that even though over the next two years I worked for that head coach, I was never late for anything involving the athletes; the fact that I lacked an understanding for why that particular behavior was important was a problem. What I would come to understand after years of blindly following leadership advice, such as never make the athletes wait for you, was that without understanding the reason why the advice was important, I was only receiving part of the lesson.

Like many young, upstart coaches, I was willing and able to comply with whatever directives my head coach gave me. I intuitively knew there was a good reason why I was being told to do it, but without asking or being told why it was important, I was missing out on keys to leadership development. It is first imperative to understand why a specific behavior is necessary. In this case, it was to set a tone and expectation that coaches and athletes were held to the same standard and expected to be on time and ready for all team activities. If, as a coach, I showed up late to a workout or community service event, I would be setting a negative example for my athletes and building in an excuse that this type of behavior was acceptable.

The second aspect of leadership development that I was missing out on was learning and having the opportunity to expand my leadership knowledge base. In this situation, I was being told by my head coach to model a specific behavior—always be on time—so that when there was an instance when an athlete was late for a team activity, I had the credibility and respect necessary to enforce the rule. Behavior modeling is a crucial aspect of any coach's leadership practice, but without understanding the concept and showing why this specific behavior was important, I was not enhancing my leadership practice, but rather mindlessly carrying out a directive. Without having a strong leadership knowledge base and understanding of leadership practice, it does not matter how much work coaches put into teaching, mentoring, advising, or being a role model for their athletes, because all those roles fall under one umbrella: leader.

Athletic coaching is an act of leadership. Coaches exhibit various leadership styles and engage in specific leadership behaviors to lead their teams to overcome adversity, foster team effectiveness, and pursue collective team goals.[1] Coaches are often given most of the credit for cultivating team success and individual team victories; however, coaches are also the ones who are usually singled out for blame when a team loses or fails to meet assigned expectations.[2] The leadership style practiced by a coach has a significant impact on the team's level of performance, as well as the team's ability to relate to the coach and form a cohesive team identity.[3]

Coaches play a crucial role in the development of their athletes. Coaches are responsible for improving athletes' physical abilities as well as psychosocial well-being. For coaches to be successful in this task, they must possess a leadership style and practice the best leadership behaviors that are most conducive to the needs of their athletes.[4] The most successful coaches are committed to leadership styles and behaviors that work toward developing an effective athlete-coach relationship and can inspire their athletes to work toward accomplishing team goals and achieving collective success.[5]

There are various definitions of leadership, but in its simplest form, I like to think of leadership as a process by which a leader (coach) unites a diverse group of individuals (athletes) so those individuals (athletes) can effectively work toward the fulfillment of team goals and expectations. That may be a simple definition, but it takes a very nuanced and in-depth understanding of leadership and leadership practice in order to achieve success within the definition's context. One of the main goals of the leadership exhibited by an athletic coach is to bring the individual talents of their athletes together so that the sum of the athletes' talents will lead to a greater chance for team success. The power to bring athletes together and rally them behind one common goal, even when that goal outshines individual accolades, is one of the most important jobs of a coach.

Coaches hold a great deal of influence over their athletes. The leadership characteristics coaches possess and behaviors they exhibit are key elements in determining whether the nature of the coach-athlete relationship is positive and contributes to the achievement of team goals.[6] In order to meet team goals and establish a level of individual commitment from each athlete who is necessary to achieve team success, the coach must use the right leadership behaviors in order to positively influence the team.[7] One of the main ways that coaches can bring individual athletes together in the pursuit of team success is through strong training and instruction and by exhibiting the positive leadership behaviors of teaching and organization in order to effectively direct athletes and build team cohesion.[8]

The influence that coaches hold over their athletes is a very important and powerful concept. An unintended consequence of coaches being asked to serve more roles is they have an increased opportunity to positively or negatively affect their athletes through their leadership choices. Leaders in fields such as corporate business, higher education, or politics require hundreds of hours of both in-house leadership trainings and professional development opportunities. But athletic coaches, whose job with each passing year more closely resembles that of a CEO or company president, do not have those same opportunities.

When I stepped on to the campus at Indiana University to start my first semester of college, I had no idea what I wanted to major in. I was always interested in history growing up and, on a whim, decided to enroll in C102 Roman History. I loved the class, enrolled in more classical studies and history courses in subsequent semesters, and graduated with a classical studies and history double major. Since graduation, I have done absolutely nothing practical with my undergraduate degree except use it as a vehicle to pursue more higher education. While surely many of my classmates either knew before they stepped onto campus or decided during their first year or two of coursework what major best fit their interests and their desired career path, I had no idea what my professional aspirations were—this made selecting a practical major impossible.

Being a classical studies and history major in college did not help me one iota when it came time to pursue my dream of being a college basketball coach. Any number of other majors would have been more beneficial for my future career, but at the time, I was eighteen years old and not thinking that far ahead. After graduation, I packed up my old red stick shift Dodge Neon and left Bloomington behind without much more than a hazy idea of what the future would hold. I knew I wanted to be a college basketball coach, but whether my efforts to make that dream a reality would amount to anything was an open question. Finally, after months of applications, emails, and phone calls, I landed a job as an assistant men's basketball coach at a small Division II school in Silver City, which is located in the southwest part of New Mexico.

When I arrived at Western New Mexico University, I was ready to take on the world. This was the first step on my path to becoming a Division I head coach and eventually joining the pantheon of legendary coaches. However, clouded by my naïveté and egotism, I was about to make a decision shortly after stepping on to campus that was not directly related to coaching but would end up altering the course of my life over a decade later. At the time, and probably still today, many Division II assistant coaches were actually graduate assistants, only with a better title. As part of my compensation, which included a small stipend, I was given room and board (i.e., a dorm room and punch card so I could eat meals in the cafeteria), and nine credits per semester of graduate tuition.

Even though I had no prior plans to attend graduate school, enrollment was a condition of the job. After arriving on campus, I scheduled an appointment with an advisor to pick a program and enroll in classes. The meeting did not take very long because after I told my advisor that I had a classical studies and a history liberal arts degree, she responded that I only had two options for a graduate program that would accept me. After my advisor laid out the required courses and timeline for graduation from the two programs, I decided to enroll in the educational leadership graduate studies program for no other reason than the counseling program required six additional internship hours beyond the thirty-six credit hours required for completing the degree.

Call it serendipity or just dumb luck that I stumbled into a graduate program centered on teaching its students about leadership and leadership practice. I had the opportunity to get a graduate degree in an area of study that had a profound impact on my ability to perform and succeed as a college basketball coach and later as a senior-level college athletics administrator. I was lucky; there is no mistaking it.

I was fortunate to receive a mulligan after not choosing an undergraduate major that would help me in my professional endeavors. But what about all the athletic coaches out there who choose different paths, ones that did not include getting a degree centered on teaching them about leadership? Without all the training opportunities afforded in other professions, how are coaches supposed to acquire the knowledge and understanding necessary to fully unlock their leadership potential and become the most effective and successful leaders?

The answer to that final question is what has driven me to conduct research in the area of athletic coach leadership practice and ultimately write this book. I have met so many coaches during my time as a college basketball coach who have modeled their leadership practice on the head coaches they worked for or from reading books by successful coaches where they explain the leadership techniques that make them successful. Undoubtedly, there are successful coaches who learned everything they know about leadership practice from the coaches they worked for, and others who modelled their leadership practice on successful coaches they did not work under. But I believe that, for most coaches, the key to enhancing their leadership practice, and becoming more effective and successful leaders, is by teaching them how to bridge the gap between their perceived and actual leadership style.

Bridging this gap is achieved by first giving coaches the knowledge base necessary for them to understand the leadership style and behaviors they want to practice, and then teaching coaches how to practice that leadership style and model those behaviors for their athletes. The most successful coaches are intentional about their leadership practice and have the knowledge base and understanding required to both practice the most effective leadership style for them and model the best behaviors for their athletes. This book will provide coaches with the tools necessary to be effective leaders and guide their athletes and teams to success.

CHAPTER I

Many researchers have studied and written about the effectiveness of various leadership styles for organization or team leaders. As a result, there is no consensus on what style leaders should universally adopt. It is my opinion, however, that leadership is the single most important factor in the success or failure of an organization or team. Leadership styles usually differentiate based on how a leader chooses to interact with and motivate their followers.[9] One of the main purposes of a leader is to influence and guide the development of their followers, and guidance can be achieved through a variety of leadership styles. However, all these leadership styles influence organizational performance and effectiveness in vastly different ways.[10] This is because no two leaders are exactly alike, and it is impossible to copy another leader's exact leadership style or approach.

Every coach has their own distinct personality and demeanor, and, therefore, every coach has their own unique approach to leadership. A coach who practices transformational leadership and is very high strung with a Type A personality will have a different impact on their athletes than a coach who also practices transformational leadership but is more reserved and calmer in their demeanor. From how coaches carry themselves to the tone of their voice impacts how athletes will receive the message being sent to them.

Over time, athletes develop an intrinsic understanding of their coaches' key leadership behaviors and approaches. Through repeated success or failure, athletes will become aware of how their coach is going to handle either situation and how the coach will respond in the aftermath of adversity or triumph. Athletes know when their coach is not acting like themselves and are acutely aware when outside factors might be affecting their coach's mood or behavior. If a coach has done their job and established a strong relationship with their athletes—a relationship that is based on trust and respect—athletes will be able to detect when their coach is not acting like themselves or acting in an unconventional manner.

I am a very calm person by nature. During my years as a college basketball coach, I rarely raised my voice or swore at my athletes, and I almost as infrequently heaped overwhelming amounts of praise on them. I was a rock, rarely ever too high or too low. I also believed that due to my calm and even-keeled personality this leadership behavior worked well for me. My athletes knew what to expect from me, and in the rare instances when I got upset or excited, my change in demeanor would have more meaning and significance due to its rarity. However, before I came to this realization that being even-keeled worked well for me as a leader, I had a real authenticity problem when it came to my athletes.

In my third year as a coach, I was an assistant at Dartmouth College, and our season got off to a rough start. Since I was still a young coach and finding my voice, I did not talk much at practice and instead spent a lot of time observing and learning from the veteran coaches on the staff. While this seemed like a good way to continue to learn and grow as a coach, some of my athletes interpreted my quiet demeanor as me being afraid to coach or to correct them. It also inadvertently led some athletes to believe that I was harboring negative feelings about them, or how they were playing, that I did not want to say in front of the other coaches.

When I was alerted to this dynamic by another assistant coach, I began racking my brain for a solution. Since we were in the midst of an early season losing streak, and I had noticed some of the athletes were beginning to get a bit frustrated with how the team was playing, I decided to combat my perception with the athletes as quiet and negative by becoming loud and positive whenever possible. During the next game, I was yelling encouraging comments from the bench as though I had become the team's head cheerleader. When the athletes walked off the court during timeouts, I would sprint off the bench and greet them by clapping and telling them they were doing great and that we were okay.

After a few more games of acting like this—and a few more losses—I decided to ratchet up my positivity another notch in an attempt to keep the athletes' spirits up and encourage them to keep fighting. Even though at the time I felt like a complete phony for acting like this—and that I was lying every time I did it because I did not usually believe the fake encouragement coming out of my mouth—I still thought this was the best way that I could contribute and change the way the athletes saw me.

Eventually, my misguided attempt to alter my personality and leadership style was exposed. During a game, one of the athletes ran up to me on his way to the bench and starting clapping in my face and saying, "We are okay, Coach. We are okay." It was a humiliating moment that I thought about continuously. If I was not comfortable acting a certain way, then I should not have done it just because I thought it would change the athletes' perception of me. That is not to say that leaders should not take risks or try different behaviors or leadership approaches, but leaders should always stay true to who they are and let that shine through their actions.

My athletes knew that I was not an exceedingly positive person who heaped praise on them for the slightest achievements. When I did, they saw right through it and eventually lost their trust in me as well as their respect for me. First and foremost, leaders must be true to themselves. While exceedingly positive leaders may need to be willing to insert more constructive critiques of their athletes into their leadership approach and vice versa, leaders should not compromise their core beliefs and personal identity in the process of altering some of their behaviors.

No person has the perfect personality or demeanor to be a leader. Every leader has shortcomings, faults, and areas of weakness. For me, it was not having yet found my voice when I started coaching at Dartmouth. But I knew that in order to coach my athletes with the passion and determination that I bottled up inside, I needed my leadership style to grow. Making changes to a coach's leadership practice takes time, and it also takes self-awareness and interpersonal reflection. One also should have a willingness to solicit advice from those who know them best, as well as the humility to receive coaching from more experienced peers without becoming defensive or being in denial.

Leadership practice does not change overnight. It is a process that starts with coaches understanding who they are as a person and a leader. It also requires coaches to know their strengths and weaknesses, and maintain the ability to learn, grow, and adapt as they progress through their career and encounter both successes and failures. I still haven't completely finished growing as a leader, and over a period of several years, I became a more positive coach who never again compromised my calm demeanor and even-kneeled personality. At Dartmouth, I tried to dramatically and rapidly change my leadership practice by yelling words of encouragement that I didn't believe to my athletes. I was correct that being more vocal and positive would help me better connect with my athletes, and therefore I would become more successful as an assistant coach. However, my strategy for altering my leadership behaviors was misguided and too accelerated. This approach left me in a worse position than when I started, because, at the beginning of the year, I was honest and true to myself by doing what I thought was right; by the end of the season, I was completely fake and did not resemble my core values at all. This was just one of my failures as a leader in the beginning of my career, and I knew from this and other experiences that I needed to reflect and change my leadership style for the better.

While multiple leadership styles have been proven to achieve the same outcomes, the situational leadership theory expands on this idea by arguing that for leaders to be effective, they must be willing to adapt or change their preferred leadership style.[11] Situational leadership is an approach that does not confine leaders to one specific method of leadership. Instead, situational leadership allows leaders to employ various methods in different situations. This approach focuses on the situation dictating or shaping the leader's behaviors and encourages the leader to be more flexible and adaptive with their leadership behaviors.[12]

Depending on the willingness and ability of the athletes, coaches need to be willing to try multiple leadership styles in order to determine the most effective one for themselves.[13] The idea that a coach needs to be adaptable and willing to try multiple leadership styles supports the assertion that one universal leadership style will not be effective for all leaders. Coaches also need to be willing, based on the needs of their athletes, to incorporate characteristics from multiple leadership styles in order to determine the best leadership approach.[14] However, for coaches to recognize the impact that certain leadership styles and specific leadership behaviors have on their athlete's satisfaction and performance, they must be willing to evaluate their own behavioral process and leadership practice on a consistent basis.[15]

While it is important for leaders to be willing to evaluate and alter their leadership practice, simply attempting to copy the leadership style and mimic the behaviors of the most successful athletic coaches is not the way to achieve long-term success. A key aspect of what makes successful coaches successful is that they have determined through education, trial and error, and other methods what the best leadership style and behaviors are for them to practice, as well as how to practice those behaviors so that they have the maximum positive impact on their athletes. This is very difficult to achieve, and often even more difficult to explain, which is why assistants who work for successful head coaches are not guaranteed to be successful head coaches themselves.

As already discussed, personality and demeanor play an important role in defining a coach's leadership style. Other factors, such as environment, the unique needs of the athletes, and the coach's values, all play a role in a coach's ability to be successful. If a coach replicates the leadership style of a successful coach, this practice can be all-consuming and cause the coach to lose their personal leadership identity or second-guess their leadership instincts. What makes the most successful coaches successful is an understanding of every step of the leadership process and how it informs every decision that they make no matter how large or small.

Far too often, leaders are judged based on the outcomes of their biggest decisions. However, the process that led to those decisions and outcomes can be more important for leaders in the long run as it illuminates what type of leader they are and where their leadership practice went right or wrong. Most people only get glimpses into the thought process behind a successful coach's biggest decisions through books or speaking engagements. This is not to say that successful coaches do not, or cannot, play a vital role in moving the leadership conversation forward by educating current and future coaches. It is impossible, however, for a coach to expect to become successful by simply copying the leadership practice of another successful coach.

What coaches who want to be successful should be trying to do with their leadership practice is not copy the most successful coaches or model their practice off them, but rather copy the process by which they transformed themselves into highly effective and enormously successful leaders. This process starts with a coach determining who exactly they are as a leader, and then identifying their leadership strengths and weaknesses. Once that has been established, a coach needs to be educated on leadership practice in order to determine the best leadership style for them to practice that does not conflict with their core beliefs or personal identity.

It was always important to me as a coach that my words and emotions had an impact on my athletes, but I also learned that athletes often respond with more sustained effort and intensity from positivity than from negativity. This was a valuable insight gained from both my educational and professional experiences, and it allowed me to realize that I was not acting true to myself as a leader when I decided to take an overwhelmingly positive approach to leadership when I was an assistant coach at Dartmouth. Over time, this approach left my positive words hollow because I doled them out for even the smallest accomplishment one of my athletes attained. As a leader, coaches must understand how to display moderation in altering their leadership behaviors so that the changes are still consistent with their identity and the leader they want to be.

An understanding of how to adapt ones' leadership style in order to maximize its impact and effectiveness is an important skill for coaches to learn. It not only allows coaches to continually evolve to meet the unique and changing needs of their athletes and team, but also to understand and be able to identify when aspects of their leadership practice are not working the way they intended and need to be altered. This skill is not complete, however, without the knowledge and understanding of how to practice specific leadership behaviors. Additionally, this skill will allow coaches to distinguish between when a leadership behavior is not working because they are practicing it incorrectly and when it is not working because it is not the best leadership behavior for them to practice based on the unique needs of their athletes.

If you have been in coaching for any length of time, you have probably witnessed or heard about a coach using negativity, specifically executing anger through degradation as a method to motivate their athletes to play harder. This motivational tactic falls in line with the belief that a segment of coaches have, which is that a certain type of athlete needs to be mad to play well. This practice, or the adoption of this practice by coaches, generally happens in times of desperation, such as when coaches are the most frustrated or fraught with self-doubt that their initial strategy for motivating their athletes is not working or was somehow wrong to begin with.

The most common scenario when I have seen this specific tactic employed is at halftime of a contest when the coach's athletes are severely underperforming in the areas of effort, intensity, and execution of the game plan. In this scenario, the team is likely losing—usually by a substantial amount—and the coach is desperate to try any leadership tactic that might help to motivate their athletes to get back on track and perform at their expected level. While this leadership behavior can produce short-term results (i.e., the team responds to the coach's outburst by getting mad and collectively deciding to play as hard as possible in an attempt to prove their coach wrong), the long-term implications of employing such a leadership behavior are overwhelmingly negative. When this tactic is employed on a routine or even infrequent basis, the results are often destructive and include the erosion of the trust previously built between the coach and their athletes, as well as the deterioration of the team's culture and values.

When I started my eighth season as an assistant basketball coach at Chicago State University, we were in the midst of three straight difficult seasons. The prevailing feeling in the coaching community was that we were on our last legs. Internally, the coaching staff collectively viewed the situation a little differently; however, speaking for myself, I was feeling more pressure to win that season than I had in any of my other seasons as a college basketball coach. When the pressure and stress that come with coaching a team— both at the amateur and professional levels— begin to seep into your leadership practice, the potential for mistakes and uncharacteristic behaviors is increased to potentially dangerous levels.

Early in the season, I noticed myself having less patience in situations where my athletes and the team were progressing slowly on the steep learning curve that is ushered in with the start of workouts and practice each year. Normally, during this time of year, I constantly remind myself to have the utmost patience when it comes to the growing pains that new athletes exhibit during their first few weeks as a member of the team. It will often take time for new athletes, and even some returners, to get acclimated to the team culture and expectations. At the start of this season, however, I was anxious for the new athletes and team to show immediate progress and signs that we were going to turn things around.

When a coach's leadership practice becomes infected by personal or outside issues, it can be exceedingly difficult to put those feelings aside and remain focused on executing leadership behaviors that are intended to motivate and inspire their athletes. If a coach is not completely confident in their leadership practice and can't give the emotional energy required to perform the necessary leadership behaviors, then the coach's leadership style will not be effective. A coach's ability to block out all the extraneous pressures and stresses, not only associated with being an athletic coach but also those that are simply a part of life, is an extremely important part of being a successful leader. Without this ability, over time—or sometimes unfortunately all at once—a coach can lose their leadership identity and perform leadership behaviors that are uncharacteristic. In some cases, this may do irreparable harm to the team and the coach's relationship with the athletes.

I did not realize it at the time, but the lack of patience I was demonstrating with my athletes was emblematic of how my leadership practice was being eroded and altered by the outside stresses I was feeling on a daily basis. When the team got off to a rocky start, my anxiety and stress levels were ramped up another notch. By Thanksgiving, I recognized changes in my leadership style. My calm and even-keeled demeanor was infected by bouts of anger and frustration that I was taking out on the athletes. I yelled corrections or criticisms instead of calmly explaining them or pulling an athlete to the side and sternly speaking to him more privately. I became more demonstrative and my infrequent words of encouragement, and positivity became almost non-existent as I held my athletes to a standard of perfection that was completely unattainable and set them up for failure.

It was Thanksgiving Day, and we were in Baltimore, Maryland, playing in an event hosted by the University of Maryland Baltimore County. The coaching staff believed that this game was the first of two that we had a great chance of winning, and if we accomplished that goal, it could be the catalyst to turn around our season. In the first game, we played the host team and struggled from the opening tip. We looked sluggish and dug ourselves into an early hole that we tried to dig out of for the entire first half. During halftime, my comments were generally positive and focused on how if the team improved their play in a few key areas, we would put ourselves in a position to comeback and have a chance to win the game.

When we started the second half with a similarly sluggish effort, my frustration instantly jumped, and as the team jogged off the court for a timeout, I could not contain my dissatisfaction any longer. Instead of walking over to talk with the other coaches about strategy before speaking with the athletes, I made a beeline for the bench and berated the athletes about their lack of effort and intensity, accusing them of not have a strong enough will to win and playing soft. This behavior was extremely uncharacteristic for me, and I saw in my athletes' eyes that they were taken aback by my aggressive tone and negative words. To make matters worse, the game was televised on ESPNU—as the timeout ended, the camera panned over to our huddle where I was dressing down the athletes for my friends, family, and everyone else watching the game to see.

In the aftermath of my outburst, the team responded by playing noticeably harder and with more intensity; however, it did not last, and we ended up losing the game by a wider margin than the amount we were losing by before my eruption. In the locker room after the game, my frustration continued to boil over, and I made more remarks to my athletes that I would later come to regret.

That night, after things calmed down, the team gathered in a banquet room at the hotel and ate a Thanksgiving meal together. There was storytelling, laughter, and a joviality that embodied all the best things about sports and being part of a team. Right before we ate, my head coach asked everyone to stand up in a circle and hold hands while we went around the room and everyone said what they were thankful for. When it was my turn, I started my remarks by saying that I was thankful for my wife and daughter and for the opportunity to be a coach and do what I loved every day. I said a few other things before closing by saying that I was thankful for the chance to be a part of a team and for the exceptional athletes I was privileged enough to coach.

The following day, on the bus heading over to play our next game, I took a seat surrounded by a several of the athletes I had been the hardest on during the previous day's game and apologized for my harsh words. It is one of my core beliefs that I must be willing to admit when I am wrong and apologize face-to-face to those I have wronged—this belief has always been an integral part of my leadership practice. I knew that I had compromised many of my core leadership values when I took my frustration out on my athletes the day before, and it was important to me that my athletes knew my actions were not representative of how I felt about them and were incited by forces that had nothing to do with them. When I finished apologizing, one of the athletes who I had recruited said that he understood what I was saying and that the team knew that in my heart I did not believe what I had said. They still believed that I always had their best interests in mind and that I wanted to see them succeed.

This was a pivotal moment for me as a leader—one that taught me an immense amount about myself and the impact I could have on my athletes as long as I stayed true to my core leadership values. When coaches have taken the time to develop their leadership style, including establishing a set of guiding core values at the foundation of their leadership practice, these values will ultimately emanate in their leadership behaviors and influence their athletes. Having this foundation is key to becoming a successful leader, because it allows coaches to have setbacks from time to time without completely and irreparably harming their relationship with the team and individual athletes. When coaches direct all their efforts and energy into doing what they believe is best, a trust will be established with their athletes that is almost impossible to break.

No leader is perfect, and no coach practices all the best leadership behaviors 100 percent of the time. However, if underlining every decision a coach makes and behavior they model is the belief that what the coach is doing is in the best interests of the athletes and team, then whether down the road that decision or action turns out to be right or wrong is not necessarily the most important thing. The process can be just as, if not more, important than the outcome, because leaders are going to make missteps and wrong decisions. As long as leaders stay true to themselves, do not try to become someone else, or allow outside factors to lead them to fundamentally compromising who they are at their core, then they will remain on the right track and continue to have what no coach can be successful without: the trust and respect of their athletes.

CHAPTER II

No leader practices only one leadership style. Some leaders may practice all the key behaviors that constitute transformational leadership, but hidden within at least a few of those behaviors are elements of other leadership styles that influence their overall leadership practice. While the list of recognized and studied leadership styles is constantly growing and evolving, the two most common styles that coaches believe they practice and actually practice are transformational leadership and transactional leadership. While transformational leadership is a very common style for leaders in areas such as education, business, and technology, athletic coaches commonly practice transactional leadership, or at least several of the key behaviors.

When assessing whether transformational or transactional leadership is better for coaches to practice, a key distinction between the two styles are their approaches to motivating followers. Both styles share the same goal—which is to inspire followers to believe in the organization and be motivated to work harder and achieve more—but they approach this goal differently. Transformational leaders help followers to cultivate goals and objectives, which is necessary for athletes who participate in team sports, while transactional leaders operate on a contingent rewards-and-punishments system that can help coaches to alter or maintain the best status quo.[16] Coaches are often viewed as inspirational motivators when a strong athlete-coach relationship has been established, and coaches have the power to use their transformational leadership abilities to help athletes reach their practice and performance capabilities by stimulating them to be more creative and innovative thinkers.[17]

The idea of coaches employing a rewards-and-punishments system to motivate their athletes is a relatable and practical idea for many coaches. Athletes or teams who underperform at practice by not focusing or giving maximum effort might receive a punishment from their coach in the form of extra running. By the coach requiring that the team or specific athlete be punished for their performance, the coach is trying to motivate their athletes to work harder or give more effort. Along these same lines, if the team is giving their all and exceeding their coach's expectations at practice, the coach might reward their athletes by ending practice early or giving the athletes extra time off the next day. Both cases might seem like cliché coaching moves that seemingly every coach has used during their career, but at the core of these behaviors is transactional leadership.

The coach-athlete relationship is influenced by the coach's specific leadership style and is also directly affected by the coach's primary leadership characteristics.[18] All athletes are different, and charisma has been identified as a leadership characteristic that is important for leaders and followers to build a promising and strong relationship. Charisma is a key characteristic of several leadership styles, including, most prominently, transformational leadership; however, charisma is also an essential characteristic of transactional leadership, although that association is not considered to be as strong as with transformational leadership.[19]

On the surface, a coach who is seen as charismatic could be a transformational or transactional leader. In such a case, the accompanying leadership behaviors, as well as their underlying core values, will indicate whether the coach is really a transformational or transactional leader. For example, if a coach uses their charisma to build up their athletes through uplifting communication and positive reinforcement, then that coach is more of a transformational leader. If a different coach uses their charisma to get the athletes to buy into a system where positive actions are rewarded and negative behaviors are punished, then that coach practices transactional leadership. In this example, two coaches sharing the same character trait have employed it in two different ways in an attempt to achieve the same basic result: inspire athletes to work harder and be motivated to give their all.

A coach understanding their strengths, such as being charismatic, is the first step to understanding which leadership style is best for them. However, a coach simply identifying the character traits that they consider strengths and the ones that are weaknesses does not alone help the coach choose the right leadership style. Perhaps that same first coach believes in using charisma to build a strong coach-athlete relationship, which has been determined to be a central component of athlete development, as positive athlete development has also been found to be a key factor in athletic team success.[20] A critical aspect of a successful coach-athlete relationship is the coach giving their athletes positive feedback and providing them with social support.[21] By providing positive feedback and social support, the coach is using charisma to lead and motivate their athletes with transformational leadership behaviors.

Another defining aspect of athletic coach leadership is influence. Coaches exert influence in order to direct athletes and to help them focus on individual improvement as well as the pursuit of team goals.[22] The second charismatic coach mentioned earlier may not see the coach–athlete relationship as being crucial to the leadership process and considers a more pragmatic approach to be more appropriate and potentially successful. This coach may believe that the pursuit and accomplishment of many short-term goals is the best way to keep athletes on track and focused on the ultimate team mission for that season. While transformational leaders focus more on long-term goals that are achieved through the effects of consistent positive communication and through giving athletes individualized consideration, transactional leaders focus on attaining short-term goals through a contingent and straightforward rewards-and-punishments system.

Even though both coaches are starting with charisma as their key leadership trait—and the coaches might very well have the same end goal for that season—the leadership style they choose will put them on very different paths. Several factors influence whether a coach's chosen leadership style is successful. One example is whether the coach has the leadership knowledge to practice the specific behaviors associated with the style they choose. Another is whether the coach truly believes and is committed to practicing those behaviors even when they do not see immediate results.

Before the 2016–2017 basketball season, I decided to try to incorporate a few new leadership behaviors that I had recently learned about into my practice. Early in my career, I gravitated toward the transformational leadership style. My leadership practice was still evolving, and I was figuring out what behaviors came naturally to me and whether they could help me be successful. It has always been my belief that a coach's job is to inspire their athletes to be greater than they ever thought they could be, and to instill in athletes the belief that they can achieve more than they ever thought they could. That is the fundamental principal of my leadership practice, and I consider it before every leadership-related decision I make.

In pursuit of this belief, I decided prior to the season to use inspirational motivation and to set high standards for my athletes—higher than the athletes thought they should be—in order to demonstrate my belief in their ability to achieve more than they thought they could. Unfortunately, as an assistant coach, the opportunities to implement a leadership approach for the entire team are limited, so I decided that I would try to use inspirational motivation on only a few of our athletes who I thought would benefit from it the most. Initially, I focused a lot of my attention on one of our sophomore athletes who was coming off of an up-and-down freshman year, but who I believed had great potential to be an integral part of the team if he had more confidence in himself and his basketball abilities.

However, it is not simply enough to decide you are a transformational leader, learn about a specific behavior such as inspirational motivation, and then attempt to practice it. I tried this approach in years past with very mixed—and often disappointing—results because I was missing a key aspect of the implementation process. In my previous attempts, I did not have a unique—or even well-developed—method of how I was going to inspire my athlete to be better. In the past, I tried being more positive and encouraging by intermittently relaying my belief in the athlete's abilities and capability to achieve more, but through repeated underwhelming results, I learned that I was missing two key ingredients to successfully practicing inspirational motivation. First, I did not have a clear message to convey to my athlete. Second, I did not convey this message consistently enough for him to fully trust my belief in him. This meant my athlete did not believe I was committed to him or invested in his improvement.

This time around, I decided that my approach would be to pick out at least one moment every day during practice or other team activities where the athlete did something I thought was exceptional and point it out in front of the entire team to help build his confidence. In addition, I would pull him aside at or near the start of every practice and tell him that I believed in him and thought he was one of the best athletes on the team, with the potential to be *the* best. These actions were crucial because they established trust and a bond with the athlete and proved that I was as invested and engaged in his improvement and reaching his potential as he was. This also established in the athlete's mind that I believed he was one of the best athletes on the team, which changed how he saw himself and increased his self-confidence.

Based on the athlete's inconsistent performance during the previous season, I knew that it would take the athlete time and commitment to improve, as well as our head coach to believe in his abilities. I have never been shy when the opportunity arises for me to speak my mind during coaching staff meetings, and I have always used those opportunities to advocate for the athletes I truly believed were putting in the effort and were committed to the achievement of team goals. After a few weeks of practice, I believed that this athlete met that standard, so I began advocating for him to get more playing time based on my belief in how good he could be. I knew it would take time, but in lock-step with the athlete's improvement, our head coach began to notice and gave him more opportunities.

Finally, in a mid-December non-conference game, the athlete was given the chance to start. He made the most of the opportunity, playing extremely well and exhibiting a team-first mentality that our head coach acknowledged in the locker room after the game in front of the entire team. The next game was three days later, and at our team practice the night before, our head coach said to me several times how confident the athlete looked and how his mentality had changed dramatically from last year and even earlier in the season. The game the following day was a tight hard-fought contest between two equally talented teams. We traded leads throughout the second half until we pulled ahead by five points with less than two minutes left. The other team did not quit, and on consecutive possessions, the other team's best player drove to the basket for an acrobatic finish, and then jumped into the passing lane to steal a pass before racing down the court to make a pull-up 3-pointer.

With the game now tied and less than one-minute left, my athlete slowly dribbled up the court as our head coach barked out instructions from the bench. Without regard for the play call or anything our head coach was saying, the athlete stepped across half-court, took a few hard dribbles toward the basket, and pulled-up from several feet behind the three-point line. As the ball left his fingertips and passed over the outstretch hands of the others team's best player—who would be playing for the NBA's Dallas Mavericks at the same time the follow year—I knew the ball was going in. As the ball passed through the net, and our team and coaches erupted off the bench, I felt pride and exhilaration swell inside me.

As a parent, I get no greater joy in life than watching my kids achieve something, especially when it is something that I know they put their heart and soul into. As a coach, there are rare moments that can summon that level of emotion and pride from an athlete's accomplishment. I was fortunate on that night to have one of those moments. The confidence that he displayed in taking that shot was incredible, but even more so when you consider the journey that he had taken from being a freshman who was unsure of his abilities to a sophomore who was willing and relished the opportunity to take a shot with everything on the line. That type of transformation is a rarity in coaching, and I felt so lucky in that moment to have been a part of his journey.

Athletic coaches, like other organizational leaders, must be encouraged to move beyond simply being managers of day-to-day responsibilities. Instead, they need to become committed to leadership.[23] By displaying strong leadership, coaches can have a positive impact on athletes' character development, self-esteem, and social skills.[24] Furthermore, the leadership impact of a coach is enhanced through a strong coach-athlete relationship. A coach having individualized consideration for their athletes can forge this relationship. Individualized consideration builds trust and leads to the athletes having a greater understanding of their coach's expectations and vision for achieving success.

A coach who practices individualized consideration is showing concern for and emphasizing athletes' individuality. However, whether a coach who practices individualized consideration is successful depends largely on the coach's ability to intellectually stimulate and guide athletes toward the achievement of individual goals that collectively contribute to greater team success.[25] All athletes have different needs; however, when it comes to their leadership practice, there are several ways that coaches can approach these differences, even when the coaches in question are all practicing the same leadership style.

Let's assume there are a group of coaches who all practice transformational leadership, and all believe it is a priority for them to inspire and motivate their athletes. It could be easily assumed that how all these transformational leaders approached motivating and inspiring their athletes would be very similar; however, that is not necessarily the case. Based on the different make-ups of each team and the personalities and needs of the individual athletes that comprise them, each coach will develop a unique approach to motivating and inspiring their athletes.

For example, one coach may decide that they are going to coach all the athletes the same way and use the same motivational and inspirational approach for each team member regardless of the individual needs an athlete might have. The coach in this example uses the same positive communication, has the same reliance on charisma, and considers themselves a role model for the athletes. However, by choosing to use the same motivational and inspirational approach for every athlete, the coach is forgoing the transformational leadership principal of individualized consideration. Another coach in this same group may have the same ideas as the previous coach, except that they decide to emphasize the individual needs of each athlete on the team and attempt to devise an approach that each unique athlete will respond to best. Neither approach is wrong, and both approaches have the opportunity to be successful. The coach needs to understand and account for the potential unintended consequences of each path, as well as believe their approach best aligns with their core leadership values and the team's needs.

The first coach who decided not to practice individualized consideration may struggle to build a strong coach-athlete relationship because they are choosing to deemphasize the individual needs of the athletes. At the same time, however, that coach may have an easier time establishing a sense of fairness and equality on the team because all athletes receive the same treatment and are praised for the same standard of accomplishment. The second coach may have the exact opposite response from their athletes. However, if one of the coach's core leadership values is to genuinely understand the needs of each athlete and be attentive and nurturing to those needs, then the unintended consequence of potentially creating a rift in the team culture due to the perception of unequal standards and treatment would be tolerable. Once again, this example harkens back to the ideas that every leader is different, and that there is not a perfect leadership style or approach that will guarantee success.

Even though my sophomore athlete did benefit from the individualized consideration that I showed him throughout the season, there were unintended negative consequences that arose. The most glaring consequence was that some of the other athletes on the team noticed and either wanted the same consideration or resented that they were not offered the opportunity to have it. Since I chose to focus my individualized consideration on a few of the athletes who I felt could most benefit from it, some athletes were upset with my approach. One athlete actually came up to me after a game while the team was standing in line at a fast food restaurant and asked me how he could get the same coaching from me that the other athletes receiving individualized consideration were getting.

As a leader, it is impossible to think of every potential consequence or side effect of your chosen leadership behaviors. However, if a coach is thoughtful about leadership practice and is committed to practicing a leadership style that aligns with their core values, then any potential issues that arise can be mitigated and overcome. For me, even though as an assistant coach I did not feel like I could give every athlete on the team the same level of individualized consideration, I did not want my decision to give it to some athletes to affect my relationships with the ones who did not receive it.

I thought about this problem for a long time before I came to the conclusion that providing individualized consideration for only some of the athletes was incongruous with one of my core leadership values. I fundamentally believe that a coach should provide the same opportunities for every member of the team to have their growth and development nurtured so that they can contribute to team success. Based on this realization, I decided that there was another way for me to practice individualized consideration in a more fair and equitable manner for all my athletes. With this alternative approach, I offered the same opportunity of individualized consideration to all the athletes on the team, but I did not make it a requirement that the athletes had to receive it, as each athlete is different and may not want to accept it.

While I did not explicitly approach each athlete and ask them if they wanted to receive individualized consideration, I was able to read either their subtle or not-so-subtle responses to receiving the individual attention from me. A few athletes responded positively to the individualized consideration I was now showing them, but most of the athletes preferred to receive the same type of coaching and attention I had been providing them prior to the change in my leadership approach. Ultimately, the most important lesson for me was that I needed to be proactive and assess how my leadership behaviors were affecting not only the athletes I was intending for them to have an effect on, but also how they were affecting the rest of the athletes, and if I needed to tweak or drastically change my approach.

No coach can honestly say that their leadership practice has remained exactly the same over a prolonged period of time. People change, and those changes affect their leadership practice. Athletes are constantly evolving, and with each new generation, athletes experience different challenges that require an adaptive leadership approach from their coaches. The environment coaches work in is always changing as different organizational leaders and support staff come and go. Despite this, coaches will never be far from the right leadership path if they remain true to their core leadership values and are committed to pursuing only leadership behaviors that directly align with those values. If coaches are unwavering in their commitment to this idea, then even when a leadership decision has unintended negative consequences, they will be able to navigate through those challenges and emerge a better and more thoughtful leader on the other side.

CHAPTER III

A ll coaches have a leadership style and a corresponding set of leadership behaviors that they consistently practice, whether they are consciously aware of it or not. The initial aim of my research in the area of athletic coach leadership practice was to determine the best leadership style and set of leadership behaviors for coaches to practice in order for them to be successful. And while my research did conclude that there is one best leadership style—and set of related leadership behaviors—for coaches to practice, a secondary aim of my research ended up being the inspiration for this book. Later in this book, I will exhaustively examine the leadership style and behaviors my research determined were best for coaches to practice. Before I delve into my research, though, I want to spend some time exploring the importance of my secondary research aim and its implications for coaches.

The secondary aim of my research on athletic coach leadership practice was to determine if there was a correlation between coaches' perceived and actual leadership styles. To answer this question, I sent out a survey that presented coaches with different leadership styles and asked them to indicate which of the styles they perceived themselves to practice. On the survey, I also gave the coaches several statements relating to leadership practice and different leadership styles, and I asked them to indicate whether they strongly agreed to strongly disagreed with the statement based on their own leadership views and core values. I then used the coaches' answers to determine their actual leadership style based on the specific behaviors that they indicated they practiced most often. Based on the results of the survey, I determined that there was a small degree of correlation between the coaches' perceived and actual leadership styles. And, when I say small, I mean very small, which meant that the gap between the coaches' perceived and actual leadership style was massive. I am talking Grand Canyon-sized, not look-across-the-lake-and-see-my-friend-waving-back-at-me, shockingly massive.

Now, this finding could mean a lot of things, but the overarching implication to me was that coaches do not have a firm grasp and deep-rooted understanding of the specific leadership behaviors that correspond to the leadership style they wish to practice. The implication of this first interpretation of the research for coaches could be the result of them receiving very little, if any, specific leadership training. In many cases, coaches may have only received basic classroom instructional, or experiential knowledge from which they can draw when deciding which leadership style they wish to practice and how to practice it. Additionally, based on the coaches' experiences and the behaviors of their coaching mentors, they may have developed a hybrid leadership style. They may not even be aware that their behaviors as leaders correspond to a specific leadership style.

As I delved deeper into the implications of my research findings, I kept coming back to the idea that a significant part of the gap between coaches' perceived and actual leadership style was the result of a lack of leadership training or knowledge. And, if coaches had easier access to training, they would be far more likely to have the knowledge base necessary to understand the leadership style or styles they practice or want to practice. This leadership knowledge would also inform the coaches of what leadership behaviors would be the most effective for them to practice and how to practice those specific leadership behaviors in order to achieve success.

Additionally, the fact that my research found there to be a very small correlation between the perceived and actual leadership style of coaches has several important implications for coaches' leadership practice. First, it could imply that coaches either do not know the specific leadership behaviors that correspond to the leadership style they wish to practice, and therefore are unable to practice that leadership style. Secondly, it could also imply that coaches know what leadership style they wish to practice and what the corresponding behaviors are for that leadership style, but they either intentionally or unintentionally do not follow through on practicing those behaviors.

The fact that there was a huge gap between the perceived and actual leadership style of coaches struck me to my very core. How can coaches be asked to wear so many hats and be responsible for influencing and shaping the development of the young people they are entrusted to coach if they are not given the necessary tools to ensure they had a fighting chance at success? The last implication of my findings was even more depressing for me, because it implied that coaches may lack an understanding of why leadership knowledge is important to their success as coaches and why the follow-through of specific behaviors is crucial to their role as leaders. Even though I do not believe this to be a likely case for most coaches, it is undoubtedly the case for some—and that is too many in my estimation.

Leadership is a central aspect of a coach's job. It is essential that coaches practice the most effective leadership style in order to help their team maximize performance and achieve success.[26] However, without leadership training and increased quality methods for coaches to obtain leadership knowledge, how can they bridge the gap that exists between their perceived and actual leadership style? The answer to that question is simply that they cannot. That is why I wrote this book. Through my research, I have developed a two-step method that will help coaches bridge the gap between their perceived and actual leadership style and become the leaders they want to be.

The first step is to provide coaches with the knowledge required to have an in-depth understanding of leadership practice, to the point where they become quasi experts in the area themselves. The second step is to then provide those coaches with practical training that explains how they can take all the knowledge and understanding they just received and put it into practice. The next two chapters of this book are going to focus on accomplishing those two steps. As I always tell my athletes and the coaches I have been fortunate to mentor over the years, identifying a problem is the easy part—the hard part is coming up with realistic solutions and a pathway to fix the problem. This has become a mantra of mine, and it actually stems from an important leadership lesson that I learned very early in my career.

The 2008–2009 basketball season was my first year as a Division I assistant coach, and, as I previously mentioned, I had some issues figuring out how to relate and coach the athletes. However, even though I did not say much to the athletes, I had no problem voicing my opinions to the rest of the coaching staff, who each had spent more years as coaches than I had spent on Earth. Thankfully, the other coaches took my youthful exuberance in stride, and the two other assistant coaches became great mentors to me over the course of the season, providing me with numerous important leadership lessons that I still incorporate as part of my leadership practice.

One such leadership lesson I learned during a trip we made to California just after Christmas to compete in a classic hosted by the University of California, Berkeley. Our season had gotten off to a rocky start, and as a way to help combat our struggles, I watched a lot of film in order to try to figure out what our team's problems were. One of the issues I found was that we relied too heavily on midrange jump shots for our offense and did not get to the free throw line enough or get enough good looks from the three-point line. The bottom line in my estimation was that we did not attack the basket enough, and as a team, we needed to have a more aggressive mindset.

During the first half of our game again the University of California, Berkeley, I noticed this problem happening again as our defense kept us in the game, but we struggled to keep pace on the scoreboard due to our offensive inefficiency. At halftime, the coaches gathered outside the locker room to discuss how the first half had gone, and I immediately chimed in with a detailed diagnosis of our offensive struggles: too many midrange jump shots, not enough free throw attempts, and too many contested looks from three-point range. If I had not been so caught up in my diatribe, I would have noticed the smoke emanating from my head coach's ears as I listed off problem after problem.

I do not know if I expected applause or some other form of adulation for my perfect analysis of our team's offensive issues, but I certainly did not expect my head coach to harshly disagree with everything I was saying and refuse to acknowledge any of my points as valid. I did not say another word for the rest of halftime, and as the team and coaches walked back out to the court for the start of the second half, one of the other assistant coaches pulled me aside.

"Matt, what the hell was that? Coach has been in the profession for longer than you have been alive. He knows what our problems are. Everyone watching the game knows what our problems are. The job of an assistant coach is not simply to diagnose and shine light on the team's problems; it is to provide solutions, or at the very least make suggests that contain ideas for how to begin to address the team's problems."

What I learned from that conversation was an extremely valuable leadership lesson: no matter what your role in an organization is, you must always be thinking of ways and working to move the team forward. I also learned that, as a leader, I needed to be able to both diagnose problems within my team as well as think critically and be willing and able to provide solutions to those problems even if there was a risk of failure. This lesson turned out to be equally important after I had conducted my research and was thinking about what practical and realistic solutions to the problems I had uncovered I could offer to coaches. The next two chapters will focus on those solutions, and how coaches can incorporate them into their leadership practice to become more effective leaders.

CHAPTER IV

This chapter defines five styles of leadership, how they compare, and the pros and cons of each. When it comes to leadership, the education process starts with a discussion of what some of the most commonly practiced leadership styles are and identifying what the core values and principles are that make each style unique. Once coaches have a better understanding of these leadership styles, they can begin to determine what leadership style they perceive themselves to be practicing. Let's start with transformational leadership.

Transformational leadership is a style that is defined by the leader's approach to inspiring and motivating followers to achieve more than they believe they can. This style is centered on the leader establishing value in their individual followers as well as outlining a clear vision and goals for followers to work toward achieving. [27,28] There are four main elements of transformational leadership: individualized consideration; inspirational motivation; idealized influence; and intellectual stimulation. Transformational leaders rely on charisma to gain their followers' trust and build their legitimacy as leaders. They believe that the power of their behavior and character is more important to leadership practice and motivating and inspiring followers than through formal rules, rigid positions, or inflexible behaviors.

A coach who practices transformational leadership focuses overwhelmingly on using positive communication with their athletes to provide inspirational motivation. Setting high expectations creates a bar for athletes to strive for that far exceeds the performance expectations that they would have set for themselves. A transformational coach is uplifting every step of their athletes' journey toward achieving the high standard set for them, and the coach works to constantly provide their athletes with a sense of purpose, such as how their improvement in certain areas will greatly help the overall team's strength.

The importance of individualized consideration for coaches who practice transformational leadership cannot be overstated. Mentoring athletes is a key component of a coach's job, and individualized consideration allows them to understand the specific needs of each athlete on the team and provide the necessary support for all athletes. A coach who believes that each athlete has a specific role to play in the team's success will work to nurture each athlete's talents, and, through individualized consideration and inspirational motivation, develop their athletes into a better version of themselves with an enhanced ability to help the team achieve success.

Intellectual stimulation and idealized influence are the two other key components of transformational leadership. While inspirational motivation and individualized consideration are more often practiced by coaches who are transformational leaders, these two components should not be cast aside. Idealized influence focuses on the leader modeling the best possible behaviors for their athletes to emulate. For many organizational leaders, this is an extremely important aspect of their transformational leadership practice, but, in my experience, it can be seen as polarizing among coaches. While many coaches believe in the importance of behavior modeling, it can be difficult for coaches to always practice the behaviors they want their athletes to practice. For example, I have known many coaches who, contrary to my first head coach at Western New Mexico University, did not mind if their athletes waited for them—the coaches believed that being late from time to time was a way to exert their authority and differentiate their personal expectations and standards from the athletes'.

While this perspective may contradict my personal beliefs about leadership practice and the importance I place on behavior modeling, I have known successful coaches who believed in this practice. For these coaches, it was about respect, and that the coaches' words and actions should be unquestioned by the athletes. This practice may not be right for all coaches, but if a coach can trace a decision or behavior back to their core leadership values and not find a conflict, then that is the right leadership path for the coach to follow.

Intellectual stimulation is probably the least commonly practiced element of transformational leadership by coaches; however, as coaches are increasingly defining themselves as teachers, this element has become more prescient to coaches' leadership practice. Challenging followers to think critically, be creative, and innovate are hallmarks of intellectual stimulation. For many coaches, the athletes' role is to take directions from the coaches and then use that information to make decisions during the game, but intellectual stimulation takes that concept much further. Independent thinking is supported, and athletes are encouraged to try new approaches to solving the problems and challenges that arise during a game. This approach to leadership can lead to increased athlete buy-in since they feel more included in the team leadership process; however, it can also lead to a questioning of coaching methods and decision-making because the athletes feel empowered in their role to speak freely and work outside of the coach's direction at times.

Based on my research, more coaches perceive themselves to practice transformational leadership than any other leadership style. For coaches who read through this section on transformational leadership practice and determine that this is the leadership style they believe they are practicing, that's great—but I encourage all coaches who believe they practice transformational leadership to still read closely and focus on the next several leadership styles I discuss. A close reading of other leadership styles may reveal that there are elements of other styles that are a part of a coach's leadership practice, which is great as long as it is recognized and understood by the coach. Having a hybrid leadership style is not a bad thing; however, just as it is crucial for a coach to understand the ins and outs of a singular leadership style in order to bridge the perceived and actual leadership gap, when more than one leadership style is important to a coach's leadership practice, it is essential that they have an in-depth understanding of all styles practiced.

Transactional leadership is another common leadership style that athletic coaches perceive themselves to practice. Transactional leadership is a style where the leader focuses on the supervision and organization of their followers. The leader also promotes a contingent rewards-and-punishments system to influence and motivate followers' performance.[29, 30] This system is something that many coaches employ as a key part of their leadership practice and can relate to from their own experiences as an athlete. When a now-coach was an athlete, if they were subjected to a rewards-and-punishments system, then it stands to reason that such an experience may have strongly impacted—or at least influenced—the now-coach's leadership style.

Additionally, the framework of the coach–athlete dynamic is

often seen as one where the coach holds the power and pulls the strings based on the athlete's work ethic, performance, attitude, and commitment to the team. Under this dynamic, it is exceedingly common for the coach to use rewards such as appointing an athlete as a starter, giving an athlete increased playing time, or doling out other smaller benefits, such as more team gear to motivate their athletes. Conversely, common punishments—such as extra running, long practices, decreased playing time, or losing a starting spot—can have a strong motivational affect for athletes. This rewards-and-punishments system is as old as sports, but a gradual shift has taken place among coaches moving away from being strictly transactional leaders. Now, coaches either incorporate elements of other leadership styles—such as transformational leadership—into their practice, or change their leadership style altogether and abandon transactional leadership.

While transactional leadership is not in danger of becoming extinct, its emphasis on rewards and punishments, athletes having to respect the team chain of command, and subjecting athletes to very specific and rigid instructions and team rules can lose traction with athletes over time. After repeated exposure to something, people will adjust. As a result, transactional leaders are banking on the fact that, through enough rewards and punishments for the same behaviors, athletes will be motivated to work hard to continue practicing the behaviors that earn them rewards while working equally hard to curb the behaviors that earn them punishments. This idea is good in theory but is complicated by the fact that people are prone to eventually tuning out language or rhetoric that they have heard repeatedly.

Transactional leaders are interested in maintaining a certain amount of status quo while transformational leaders are forward-driven. Transactional leaders believe that an incremental approach to achieving goals, based on the leader telling the followers what do to and how to do it, is the best approach for moving a team forward.

If the athletes do not conform to the behavioral expectations of the transactional leader, then they will be punished, but when expectations are met or exceeded, the athletes receive rewards. Efficiency and productivity are key characteristics of transactional leaders, and coaches who practice transactional leadership may view themselves more as a manager who keeps the team on course rather than an inspirational mentor who encourages athletes to be creative and innovative thinkers.

It is common for transformational coaches to utilize a rewards-and-punishments system on occasion as a way to motivate their team and keep their athletes from becoming complacent. At one of the previous schools where I was an assistant men's basketball coach, I would occasionally watch the women's basketball team practice. The head women's basketball coach was extremely successful and modeled what a transformational leader looked like most of the time. Except, every so often when one of his starters was not performing up to his expectations that day—or had not been for a few days—he would suddenly stop practice and have her flip her practice jersey to the reversible color and join the second string. This act was not only a punishment for the starter, but also a reward for the second-string athlete who had been working hard and deserved recognition.

Through repeated observations of this exercise, I noticed that the introduction of this rewards-and-punishments system into the team dynamic not only served to motivate and inspire the first team athlete who had been punished and the second team athlete who had been promoted, but also the rest of the team who now believed that their position could shift at any time. This is a prime example of how a coach who practices transformational leadership can also incorporate transactional leadership principles into their leadership practice on occasion in order to get their athletes' attention and make an impactful point. Even though coaches far more commonly perceive themselves to practice transformational leadership than transactional leadership, a large pool of the coaches in my research study actually practiced transformational leadership in combination with another leadership style. These styles are often transactional leadership and the style I am going to discuss next: autocratic leadership.

The perception surrounding autocratic leadership is that it is a negative or inherently bad leadership style for coaches to practice. However, when coaches are completely honest about their leadership practice, it turns out that many of them practice autocratic leadership behaviors in combination with another, more pronounced leadership style. Autocratic leadership is where the leader is the sole decision-maker, and the leader draws a clear distinction between the role of the leader and the role of the followers. Within the autocratic leadership organizational structure, followers understand that all decisions must be made by the leader in order for the leadership to be effective.[31]

Many coaches perceive themselves to be the sole decision-maker for their team and solicit little input from their athletes when it comes to making team decisions. Coaches often draw clear distinctions between their role as the leader and the athletes' role as the follower. This is traditionally done by the coach telling the team that their decisions are final, and that decisions are made for the good of the team and not for the individual. On a certain level, this idea makes perfect sense for coaches, considering that if the team underperforms, the coaches are much more likely to lose their jobs than the athletes are to be dismissed from the team or traded. With so much riding for the coaches' careers and livelihoods with each team decision, it stands to reason that they would want to maintain as much control as possible over every decision no matter how big or small.

The problem with this approach to leadership is that if all the authority and control rest with the coach, then it can be exceedingly difficult for a coach to get their athletes to completely buy in to the team concept. Since the athletes have little input, they may feel a lack of ownership; this can lead to complacency and unrest, especially if the team struggles and it becomes easy to point the blame at the coach who made all the decisions that led to those struggles. However, in times of unrest, centralizing authority behind one individual can help calm the situation and take pressure off of the team to solve its problems collectively. One, clear leadership voice can help establish and maintain team stability. Long term, however, this dynamic is hard to maintain unless great success is achieved, and as a result, it is hard for the followers to question or express concern about their lack of input.

Just as with transactional leadership, autocratic leadership is structured around the coach's vision for the team, and the coach dictates to the athletes how to do things and when to do them with little or no input from the athletes. Once again, this approach contrasts the transformational leadership belief that leaders must work to motivate and inspire their athletes through innovative and creative thinking. Whereas transformational leaders deemphasize the directional nature of the coach-athlete relationship—where the coach dictates to the athlete—autocratic coaches believe they know best and that their athletes should follow their directions and lead without question. It can be hard to argue this point—after all, coaches are hired to make important team decisions and use their knowledge and experience to lead the team, but that does not mean that input from the athletes would necessarily erode the coach's power or undermine their authority.

Unlike transactional leadership where the coach uses a rewards-and-punishments system to motivate their athletes, a coach who practices autocratic leadership dictates to their athletes what do to and how to do it and then expects the athletes to follow through on those instructions to the best of their abilities.

In this scenario, the autocratic coach positions themselves as the unquestioned authority, most knowledgeable, and most experienced member of the team. With that dynamic established, the coach expects the athletes who want to improve and help the team will unquestionably listen to the coach's instructions and directives.

However, the same message or motivational tactic from one person repeated over time to a group can become exhaustive—this is the same case with the transactional leadership style. That is why it is common for coaches to practice one or two specific elements of autocratic leadership, such as being the sole decision-maker and limiting the input from the athletes, in combination with elements of transformational or another leadership style. A hybrid of autocratic leadership and another leadership style, such as transformational or transactional, helps decrease the chances that the athletes will feel disconnected from having a lack of input into team decisions or feel like their voice is not being heard.

A leadership style that is often invoked in the argument against autocratic leadership is democratic leadership, because almost all its key elements are the opposite of autocratic leadership. Democratic leadership is where the leader actively seeks the input and advice from followers in order to make organizational decisions. This practice creates an organizational culture where followers are motivated by their enhanced standing to work harder and share in organizational success.[32] These key elements all fall in stark contrast to autocratic leadership and some elements of transactional leadership.

From my research, I determined that while a significant portion of coaches perceived themselves to practice democratic leadership or democratic leadership in combination with another leadership style, a small number of coaches were found to actually practice democratic leadership or elements of it combined with another leadership style. On the surface, this finding was curious: Democratic leadership is a very popular leadership style in many other professions where organizational leadership is essential; however, the more I thought about it, the more the research findings made sense for athletic coaches.

When a coach is given the definitions of a democratic leader and an autocratic leader, it is easy to see why a coach might naturally gravitate toward the more inclusive-sounding democratic definition over the more rigid autocratic definition. Based on the research, there appears to be a stigma surrounding coaches identifying themselves as more autocratic leaders than democratic. Additionally, when the two leadership styles are explained side by side to athletes, it is predictable that they would prefer the style where they had more input into decision-making and the freedom to express their thoughts, feelings, and opinions. However, that does not mean that democratic leadership is better for coaches to practice than autocratic leadership. As previously stated, if coaches are hired as knowledge experts who are supposed to lead and make important team decisions, then, theoretically, coaches would be better off making decisions themselves and exerting their authority instead of delegating a portion of it to the athletes who likely do not have the requisite experience and knowledge base to heavily contribute to the decision-making process.

For some coaches, this may be a morose or antithetical perspective to take since athletes are the ones actually competing, and, therefore, should have some input into the decision-making process, or at least be able to have their opinions heard and considered by their coaches. From an athlete's perspective, I can completely understand why democratic leadership is appealing— for coaches who have not fully considered or fleshed out the nuances of their leadership practice, I can also see why they would be more apt to see themselves as democratic rather than autocratic leaders. It is important to many coaches that they be liked and respected by their athletes, and a democratic coach is going to have an inherently better chance at getting their athletes to buy-in to the team concept in the long-run if they feel like they have ownership and are a part of the decision-making process.

While autocratic leadership may be more effective for the achievement of short-term goals, democratic leaders are far more likely to find themselves in a situation where they are either successfully working toward the achievement of long-term goals or are stuck in neutral because the decision-making process has become too convoluted and crowded for the process to be efficient and effective. However, if a democratic leader can navigate the potential challenges of a participatory decision-making process, the upside could be higher productivity, better morale, and increased efficiency for many or all members of the team. This is no small upside and has the potential to be enormous if the leader can effectively navigate through the entire season avoiding the aforementioned pitfalls of democratic leadership.

Democratic leaders must be excellent communicators, have a strong sense of fairness, and have the courage to be open and honest about the decision-making process to allow for maximum participation. Democratic leaders must also be willing to stand up for the minority and ensure that all voices are heard, respected, and considered by the team before decisions are made. This is no small task, and with the different needs, perspectives, and agendas of the athletes, there is opportunity for the decision-making process to stall or consistently fall in line with the opinions and wants of the vocal majority. In these cases, it is imperative for the coach to display a willingness to jump in and unilaterally make decisions to reset the decision-making process and keep the team on track to achieving its goals.

Democratic leadership is most commonly and effectively practiced by coaches who have teams with strong athlete leadership dynamics, as, in these cases, the athletes are more willing to fall in line behind one or two athletes' voices as opposed to all members of the team standing up and expressing their individual opinions. Democratic leaders also strive in circumstances where there is a substantial amount of time to make decisions; however, in times when quick decisions need to be made, autocratic leaders who have already centralized their authority are better equipped to act quickly.

The democratic leadership versus autocratic leadership debate is a very difficult one. There are many pros and cons to both leadership styles, and the key elements of both styles are often in direct contrast to one another. For this reason, it is so important for coaches to have a firm grasp of both leadership styles. Even though some coaches may gravitate toward one style over another, they should still be able to utilize the other style when necessary.

The last leadership style that I am going to discuss in this chapter is laissez-faire leadership. Laissez-faire leadership is a style where the leader consciously decides to take a hands-off approach to leadership with the belief that followers understand their particular role within the organization, and, therefore, active leadership and oversight is unnecessary.[33] Unlike autocratic leaders who centralize all the decision-making authority within themselves and democratic leaders who encourage participation in the decision-making process from their followers but ultimately still make the final decision, the laissez-faire leader takes a hands-off approach and leaves decision-making and other important leadership functions in the hands of their followers.

Whereas democratic leadership is considered participatory because followers are encouraged to be engaged in the decision-making process, a key element of laissez-faire leadership is delegation. Laissez-faire leadership takes democratic leadership's approach that allows followers to participate in the decision-making process to another level, because laissez-faire leaders delegate to their followers and allow them to make team decisions. This leadership style is very uncommon for athletic coaches, and it is generally highly discouraged because the idea of a coach delegating decision-making to the athletes is almost counterintuitive to the defined role of the coach.

However, some coaches do identify with certain behaviors exhibited by laissez-faire leaders—particularly the hands-off approach to leadership, which is when the coach provides the proper tools and support, enabling the athletes to grow and develop more quickly as leaders. Within this leadership role, athletes are trusted to make decisions that will have a real and substantive impact on the team's ability to be successful and accomplish goals. Additionally, athletes are empowered to solve individual and team problems with little interference from the coach, which can enhance team camaraderie and build better team chemistry. Unfortunately, laissez-faire leaders all too often fall short of these outcomes, and instead productivity and morale are low due to a lack of direction and team success.

Whereas youth, high school, and college coaches may be reluctant to practice laissez-faire leadership behaviors, believing that their athletes need more oversight and direction, professional coaches are far more likely to exhibit laissez-faire leadership behaviors due to the highly advanced skill levels, intellect, and leadership abilities of their athletes. In this case, the athletes may have increased motivation to succeed since they are the ones making the decisions and therefore will feel more criticism and ownership if the decisions do not work out as intended. Additionally, on a professional team, there is usually more of a defined athlete hierarchy within the team, and an intrinsic system for defining athletes' individual roles, which can lead to greater efficiency and the ability for the team to make the best decisions with little input or oversight from the coach.

For youth, high school, or college teams where the athletes might still be in the developmental phase of their skills, knowledge, and leadership abilities, laissez-faire leadership would not be the best approach, as the athletes are not individually or collectively equipped to make the best decision for themselves and the team. For these types of teams, when it comes to decision-making and oversight, democratic or autocratic leadership would be better styles for the coach to practice. Their style should depend on the coach's personal core leadership values and beliefs regarding whether decision-making should rest solely with the coach or whether the athletes should be allowed an opportunity to participate in the decision-making process.

The intention of this chapter was to fulfill step one of the process to bridge the gap between coaches' perceived and actual leadership style. This chapter contained an examination of five different leadership styles and their key elements. A coach reading through this chapter should be able to align their perceived leadership practice with several of the key elements discussed therein. Based on the key elements that the coach identified as being part of their leadership practice, the coach will then be able to identify what leadership style or styles they perceive themselves to practice. In the next chapter, I will take on step two of the process by breaking down each of these leadership styles—as well as several other hybrid leadership styles—using practical examples to help coaches determine the leadership style they actually practice. Once a coach's actual leadership style is determined, the bridge from the coach's perceived to their actual leadership style will be built, allowing the coach to take the knowledge they have acquired during the first leadership education step and apply it to the practical examples discussed in step two. The bridge created between the two steps allows coaches to use their newly acquired leadership knowledge to enhance their leadership practice and become a more effective and successful leader.

CHAPTER V

A thletic coaches practice very specific leadership behaviors that, whether they intend to or not, correspond to a specific leadership style or hybrid leadership style. A coach may practice all the behaviors associated with transformational leadership, and, therefore, determine that they are a transformational leader; however, most coaches' leadership practice will not be that straightforward, and that's perfectly fine. Understanding both the key elements of different leadership styles and athletic coach specific behaviors allows for coaches to align their perceived and actual leadership style. Once coaches have an in-depth understanding of leadership practice and understand the essential differences between various leadership styles, they will be able to determine the leadership style they want to practice. Additionally, after coaches have been exposed to different coach-specific leadership behaviors that correspond to different styles, they will be able to match the leadership behaviors they actually practice to the style it resembles the most. At that point, coaches will have the knowledge base and in-depth understanding of leadership practice to allow them to make changes to their actual leadership style so that they can become the leader they want to be. When coaches align their perceived and actual leadership styles, they will be practicing the leadership behaviors that correspond to the leadership style they want to practice. This alignment will allow coaches to have command over their leadership practice and be the most effective and successful leaders possible.

Since the leadership style that coaches perceive themselves to practice most often is transformational leadership, let's begin by diving into transformational-specific behaviors. A common phrase in athletics is "play to your strengths," and for coaches, this can be interpreted as "play up your athletes' strengths, and try to disguise or shield their weaknesses until such a time as those weaknesses have been worked on and are no longer considered liabilities." There are a myriad of ways that coaches attempt to enhance their athletes' strengths, but transformational leaders rely specifically on personal influence and relationship building rather than on position or title to get athletes to complete sport-specific tasks that will enhance their abilities. The extent to which a coach relies on their personal relationships, developed over time and based on trust and respect, to influence their athletes' sport-specific behaviors corresponds to the coach's commitment to transformational leadership.

If a coach believes that their position as the team leader should be unquestioned—and that based on this established team hierarchy athletes should automatically give the coach their trust and respect—then that coach is not subscribing to transformational leadership. If a coach not only wholeheartedly believes that personal relationships are key to enhancing athletes' abilities but also believes that a coach should make every effort to develop strategies to enhance their athletes' performance and commitment to team improvement, then that coach is undeniably orienting their leadership practice to transformational leadership.

Coaches who are transformational leaders are constantly

looking for ways to develop the strengths of their athletes as a method for establishing continuous team improvement. The practical thinking behind this concept is that if the individual parts (athletes) each improve, then the ceiling for the sum (team) of those parts will also move in an upward trajectory. However, when practicing transformational leadership, coaches must pay close attention and give special care in order to ensure that each athlete they are working to improve on an individual level is progressing within the established team framework.

In my experience, it is helpful for coaches who practice transformational leadership and find themselves in this scenario to work in a pragmatic step-by-step fashion so that they can always keep the overall team goals and vision in mind when developing strategies for athlete and team improvement. For example, when I became the defense coordinator on our basketball staff at Chicago State and was responsible for developing and implementing our team defensive approach and strategy, I determined that the first step to improving our defense was to use my relationships I had developed with the athletes to instill a mentality that defense was important. I knew that if the athletes were committed to a defensive mentality, and if I worked to enhance each athlete's defensive strengths, then the defensive framework I was trying to build would improve.

At first, I tried to incorporate new defensive drills into our practices and workouts that were designed to improve specific aspects of defense, such as foot speed, lateral movement, and reaction time. I leaned heavily on my personal relationships with each athlete in order to instill the right defensive mentality and change the team's culture and attitude toward defense. This was a process that took time, patience, and commitment. It was also a developmental progression that relied on my ability to continually assess the individual athletes' and team's progress and be willing to adapt my transformational leadership approach when improvement slowed or plateaued. We started off the season with a tremendous defensive effort against the University of Wisconsin, who, at the time, was one of the most efficient offensive teams in the country and a great three-point shooting team. In our next game, we had a huge defensive setback against Oakland University. From that point on, we continued to show overall improvement compared to past years. At about the quarter mark of the season, we had back-to-back tremendous defensive efforts against Saint Louis University and Northwestern University on the road, and I knew we were really making great defensive strides.

One of the most difficult aspects of coaching is determining the right time to make a change or tweak an already successful process in order to continue evolving and stay ahead of the curve. This can be done strategically by changing or altering an offensive or defense strategy, but it can also be done by a coach altering their leadership approach in order to keep the athletes from becoming complacent with recent success. Determining the right moment is tricky, and it is all too often that coaches experience failure the first time they find themselves in this moment rather than success. For me, this specific moment brought more failure than success after I decided to adjust my transformational leadership approach to coaching defense and instead incorporate principles of democratic leadership into my practice.

A coach changing or altering their leadership style may or may not be an intentional or deliberate action. In my case, it was some of both. The seed for adapting my leadership practice was planted and began to grow during my conversations and individual meetings with the athletes. These interactions had been the time when I would work on building relationships with my athletes, but over time, these conversations—which previously were seldom about basketball—shifted to the topic of defense. On one hand, I achieved my goal of building a defensive mentality where the athletes cared about defense and were committed to improving;

on the other hand, I failed to establish the necessary boundaries in my relationships with the athletes that would have kept me from adopting a democratic-transformational leadership approach when I was not ready or fully committed to it.

Even though I didn't fully believe it was the right approach, I began providing opportunities for my athletes to be involved in decision-making during our conversations. While I saw this as an opportunity to serve as a mentor and teacher to the athletes during this time of change in our defensive scheme and principles, I was also fundamentally changing my leadership style. I had always been interested in the key democratic leadership behavior that coaches should be open to athletes' ideas, yet they should guide athletes to become stronger and more focused. When those ideas began to influence the decisions I made as a coach and the strategies I implemented to improve my athletes and the team, my leadership style shifted from transformational leadership to a transformational-democratic hybrid leadership style.

This would not have been a problem except for the fact that I still perceived myself to be practicing transformational leadership even though I was actually practicing democratic-transformational leadership. I had unknowingly created a gap in my perceived and actual leadership style, and this led to our defensive results mirroring the inconsistency of my leadership practice. One day I would take the athletes' ideas into account, incorporating them into the way I led and how I structured the defensive elements of practice. The next day I would revert back to relying on my personal relationships with the athletes in order to get them to focus and buy-in to the defensive principles and strategies I had decided were best for the individual athletes and team to implement.

Had I been intentional in my leadership practice and decided that it was the right time to adjust my style from transformational leadership to democratic-transformational leadership, continued defensive improvement would not have been guaranteed; however, through intentional decision-making, leaders give themselves the best chance for success when their perceived and actual leadership styles are aligned. This alignment helps navigate or mitigate unintended consequences from a leadership style change or adjustment because it allows coaches to have consistency in their leadership practice, and, as a result, coaches can identify areas that are not working optimally or at all. As coaches grow through the acquisition of leadership knowledge and experience, it is inevitable and healthy for their leadership style to change. However, it is imperative that changes to a coaches' leadership style are on their own terms and support the goals and vision they have set for the team.

In the previous example, I unknowingly adjusted my leadership practice, which led to a halt in improvement and inconsistent results thereafter. In retrospect, if I had decided that it was the right time to adjust my leadership style, I would have been better served incorporating key aspects of autocratic leadership into my transformational leadership practice instead of democratic leadership. In this situation, I was confident in the progress the team was making defensively and could have been better served adopting an autocratic-transformational leadership style in order to firmly establish my position as unquestioned leader of the defense, especially since I had already built strong foundational relationships with the athletes.

Autocratic-transformational leaders are responsible for providing goals and setting standards for the team, thereby allowing athletes to work toward achieving those goals while making sure to offer the athletes feedback concerning their efforts. Coaches should also retain control of decision-making, but they should encourage high morale so that athletes do not feel negatively affected during times of change. Had I incorporated these key elements of autocratic-transformational leadership into my leadership practice instead of veering into democratic-transformational leadership, I would have been able to relax my authority and rely less on the personal relationships I had already built with the athletes as a method to ensure continued buy-in. By practicing autocratic-transformational leadership, I would have potentially been able to achieve continued defensive improvement through a slightly different approach that kept my message from becoming stale or losing traction.

The differences in behaviors that indicate whether a coach is more democratic or autocratic might seem slight, or at times even inconsequential, but a coach's decision to be more autocratic or democratic can have a significant impact on their ability to lead successfully. In this section, I will take an in-depth look at the specific behaviors that define autocratic and democratic leadership so that coaches can establish which camp their leadership practice resides in or if they have a toe in each pool. While it is very common for coaches to practice transformational leadership in combination with either autocratic or democratic leadership, I believe it is fundamentally important that the integral behaviors of both leadership styles are viewed under a microscope. Through this assessment of both leadership styles, coaches will be able to connect or contrast their leadership behaviors with both leadership styles without the influence of transformational leadership behaviors muddying the waters.

The leadership question of whether a coach should be more autocratic or democratic is a very important one, and it really comes down to a coach's belief of how much influence athletes should have in team decisions, shaping the team culture, and contributing to the team's goal setting and establishing a vision for the entire program. For coaches practicing democratic leadership, they will believe that coaches should give their athletes authority to make, or have significant input into, important team decisions. Additionally, democratic leaders will subscribe to the belief that coaches should seek input from their athletes when formulating policies and team rules, as well as procedures for implementing them.

Now, for a portion of coaches reading those last two democratic leadership elements, their eyes will have rolled into the back of their head at the thought of athletes having that much power and influence over how the team is run and its direction, but remember: leaders can identify as having a specific leadership style without fully committing to practice the extreme elements of that style. Conversely, those coaches who read the two democratic leadership elements and related to them will probably have a similar reaction when they read two of the key elements of autocratic leadership.

Coaches who practice autocratic leadership believe that they are ultimately responsible for whether their team achieves its defined goals. Additionally, coaches are the sole decision-makers and should assign specific tasks to direct their athletes in order to achieve specific established goals.

For the coaches who read those elements and believe they are crazy because they do not allow for any input from the athletes and may contribute directly to the subversion of athlete buy-in, I would also remind you that there is always flexibility in leadership practice and a way to adjust specific leadership behaviors to achieve a desired outcome.

The last significant contrast between autocratic and democratic leadership is that coaches who practice autocratic leadership believe they should make quick decisions in times of urgency and be more deliberate in making decisions during times of less urgency. Meanwhile, coaches who practice democratic leadership believe they should have conversations or meetings with their athletes to obtain their input before taking corrective action. Clearly, coaches who practice purely autocratic leadership have a very different perspective and belief system than democratic leaders when it comes to how team decisions should be made and their approach to handling and distributing authority. After reading this section, some coaches may determine that their actual leadership style falls clearly in line with democratic leadership while others will align their leadership practice with autocratic leadership.

However, there is another camp of coaches who, after reading this section, will take stock of their leadership practice and realize they currently practice elements of both leadership styles. Practicing elements of both autocratic and democratic leadership is perfectly alright; however, I would encourage those coaches to be very careful and consider experimenting with both styles individually in order to determine which one best aligns with their personality and core leadership beliefs. While it is very common for coaches to have a hybrid leadership style like autocratic-transformational or democratic-transactional—which will be discussed in the next section of this chapter—leadership styles that pursue the same outcome through opposite means are hard to blend into an effective hybrid leadership style.

One example is a coach attempting to blend transactional leadership with transformational leadership into a hybrid style. While this is not an impossible task, if the two leadership styles are competing in terms of each styles' approach to motivating athletes, it can be difficult to blend the two styles successfully. For example, it can be viewed as counterintuitive to combine the rewards-and-punishments system of transactional leadership with the inspirational motivation core element of transformational leadership, because, in doing so, coaches might very well be cancelling out many of the positive effects of each style. A rewards-and-punishments system on its own is a mechanism for inciting change in or motivating people; therefore, if coaches who already had this system in place decided to also practice positive communication and inspirational motivation, they would be undercutting their ability to effectively punish athletes for negative behaviors or outcomes. Similarly, coaches cannot effectively be the sole decision-maker and centralize their authority while also allowing athletes to be a part of the decision-making process. If a coach did this, then it would be easy for athletes to see their collaboration as disingenuous and that the coach was not really taking their opinions and thoughts into account.

No coach's leadership style is going to be perfect or perfectly align with the needs of all their athletes, and a coach should not try to be a perfect leader or find the perfect leadership style. Oftentimes in life, more can be learned from failure than success. As leaders, this is true if coaches are willing to take a critical look at themselves and admit their mistakes or missteps with an eye toward taking steps to become better moving forward. One way that coaches restrict their ability to critically assess their leadership practice and improve from their mistakes is by trying to practice too many leadership styles at once in order to meet the specific needs of every athlete.

The problem with this approach is that the coach's leadership practice becomes convoluted, and it is nearly impossible to discern what behaviors that correspond to which leadership style are the most effective and working for most of the athletes. Without understanding what behaviors are effective, a coach cannot adjust or change their practice in a meaningful way so that it is eventually as effective as possible for all athletes. Lastly, unless coaches give specific leadership behaviors a chance to stand on their own so they can determine each behavior's effectiveness without influence or obstruction from other competing behaviors, coaches will not be able to truly know whether a specific leadership behavior was right for them and their athletes.

As much as leadership styles can be fluid and change from year to year, a coach must first establish the behaviors that align with their personality and core leadership values. Once those behaviors are established, coaches can change or alter their leadership practice as necessary based on their athletes' needs or their own changing belief system. If a coach believes that athletes should have input into the team decision-making process, then that coach should practice democratic leadership and not worry about whether that approach is best for every athlete. In the end, if a leadership behavior is not right for the leader and the leader does not fully believe in it, then it will never be right for their athletes.

Transformational leadership is popular among current coaches, but over the decades, transactional leadership has stood the test of time as one of the most common leadership styles that has key behaviors still practiced today. Coaches who practice transactional leadership rely on a contingent rewards-and-punishments system to motivate their athletes. If a coach makes it a point to reward their athletes for contributing to the achievement of team goals and standards, or punishes athletes for failing to meet team goals and standards, then that coach is practicing the most fundamental leadership behavior of transactional leadership.

When I started my first college coaching job straight out of undergrad at Western New Mexico University, I did not know what leadership style I practiced—or should practice, for that matter. I did, however, have it in my head that I needed to establish firm boundaries with the athletes and make sure that they respected my authority. Not long after the school year started, my head coach went out of town on a recruiting trip and left me and the other assistant coach in charge of the team, making sure the athletes still attended class, study hall, team workouts, and conditioning.

During the first afternoon that we were in charge, three of our upperclassmen were late for open gym. Seeing an opportunity to punish these three athletes for not meeting team standards by showing up late and exert our authority in the process, we decided to stop open gym and make the three upperclassmen run while the rest of the team watched. The three upperclassmen took their punishment without complaint, and after open gym, all three upperclassmen came to our office and apologized for being late and for setting a bad example for the younger athletes on the team. In this moment, I felt like a coach who had made a difference by positively influencing his athletes' behavior and couldn't wait to tell my head coach when he got back.

When my head coach returned to campus, he called me and the other assistant coach into his office to ask about how things went, and we told him what happened and how we handled it. After hearing the story, I looked into his eyes expecting to find pride that his young mentees were already having a positive impact on the athletes. Instead, I saw anger. He responded by telling us that coaches cannot be at open gym and that open gym cannot be mandatory; therefore, by us being there in the first place and then by having those three upperclassmen run for being late, we had committed an NCAA violation.

From a leadership perspective, I failed on several accounts, including the fact that I should have known my actions were against NCAA rules. However, aside from the embarrassment I felt from committing an NCAA violation, I would soon come to feel shame from my leadership actions. Not long after this incident, I learned about transactional leadership in one of my Educational Leadership graduate classes and realized that, through my actions, I was abusing my position as a leader. While transactional leaders do operate on a rewards-and-punishments system, I had not thought about any mechanisms for rewarding my athletes for fulfilling team goals and meeting team standards. Additionally, I had failed to let my athletes know what to expect as a reward for achieving defined goals and what the punishment would be for failing to achieve them. I had not considered that these three upperclassmen had not had any issues with lateness prior to this incident, or that my punishment may have been too severe.

Worst of all, I had attempted to use my leadership as a way to display and exert my authority over the athletes without laying the groundwork for my authority by establishing that their negative behaviors would be met with consequences and positive behaviors rewarded. It is unfair to the athletes, and the leader is ultimately going to be unsuccessful if they try to establish a rewards-and-punishments system without any clearly defined parameters or expectations. I was setting my athletes up for failure by punishing them primarily as a way to display that my authority as a leader should not be questioned.

When I realized my mistake, I decided that the rewards-and-punishments system was still the right leadership approach for me, but that before I could truly put it into place, I needed to earn back the trust of my athletes by showing compassion and a willingness to listen. This form of charismatic leadership is essential to transactional leadership—I just did not have the experience or leadership knowledge base to know how charismatic leadership traits needed to go hand-in-hand with the establishment of the rewards-and-punishments system. I also skipped the step of establishing expectations and clearly defining team goals, which is crucial to a coach becoming an effective transactional leader, because in that step is where the coach gains a lot of their credibility and trust from the athletes.

Without this step, athletes will be more likely to focus on how they have been wronged or unfairly treated by their coach, rather than understanding and accepting their punishment. It is through the understanding and accepting of punishments that coaches who practice transactional leadership hope their athletes will be motivated to improve or change negative behaviors. In this same way, rewards incentivize athletes to continue positive behaviors and allow the coach to show appreciation and encouragement for the accomplishment of individual and team goals. Athletes being rewarded and punished by their coaches has persisted for decades at all levels of sports, and it is unlikely that some form of a rewards-and-punishments system will not be relevant in sports for decades to come. It is incumbent on the coaches who practice transactional leadership in the years ahead to fully understand and be committed to the nuances of transactional leadership and be very careful in how they deploy their authority when handing out punishments. Handling a situation where athletes are punished without a deft and thoughtful hand can lead to the erosion of trust and respect from the athletes and lead to a coach's authority being undermined.

A coach must be aware of—and understand—the potential pitfalls and unintended consequences of practicing transactional leadership in combination with autocratic or democratic leadership behaviors. A coach who practices transactional leadership in combination with democratic behaviors will be comfortable working with athletes and be able to seek their input in making decisions while providing incentives and disincentives for the quality of their performance in team-related activities. When democratic leadership behaviors are incorporated into a transactional leader's practice, the result is a rewards-and-punishments system that is shaped by both the coach's expectations and the athletes' opinions or responses to the rewards and punishments. This does not mean that athletes should choose their own rewards and punishments, but by gauging the athletes' reactions to a specific punishment or reward in determining its effectiveness, the coach is allowing the athletes to have influence in the rewards-and-punishments system.

During the decision-making process, democratic-transactional coaches will discuss issues with all their athletes while considering which incentives and disincentives should be used in response to the quality of their athletes' performance during team activities. Democratic-transactional coaches will also be concerned about building consensus among all athletes on the team while making sure their athletes understand the timelines, benefits, and penalties associated with team goals. The incorporation of democratic leadership behaviors into a coach's transactional leadership practice builds on the idea that the rewards-and-punishments system is more effective when the athletes have input in the process and the athletes' feelings and opinions are considered by the coach.

This model for achieving success through a rewards-and-punishments system is in stark contrast to a transactional leader who also practices autocratic leadership behaviors. A coach who practices autocratic-transactional leadership will have responsibility for decision-making and provide incentives and disincentives for their athletes with respect to their performance during team activities. The key difference from democratic-transactional leadership is that an autocratic-transactional coach is the sole decision-maker who lets the athletes know the parameters of the rewards-and-punishments system but does not ask for the athletes' input or consider their unsolicited opinions or feelings.

Looking inward instead of outward for advice and input on team decisions is a fundamental difference between autocratic and democratic leadership. Autocratic-transactional leaders acknowledge that, as the final decision-makers for the team, they will get most of the credit or blame for decisions related to the team; therefore, they make sure that their promises for rewards and punishments made to their athletes are kept. A coach who practices transactional leadership believes that a rewards-and-punishments system is the best way for them to achieve desired positive outcomes and change negative ones. If these outcomes are going to be a measure of whether the coach's decisions were correct or incorrect, then the coach should work to keep the system intact.

Democratic-transactional leaders undoubtedly believe that they will receive a disproportionate amount of praise or blame for team decisions; however, they are committed to including input in those decisions from the athletes. Whereas autocratic-transactional leaders are willing and able to make quick decisions when necessary because they do not need to solicit input from the athletes, democratic-transactional leaders are better suited to gathering information and making a collectively informed decision over an undefined period of time. For athletic coaches, there are times when quick decisions are required and other times when a collective information gathering process might yield a better decision and outcome. Whether a coach practices democratic-transactional or autocratic-transactional leadership, it is important that the potential shortcomings of practicing either leadership style are considered by the coach.

An autocratic-transactional coach might decide to look at certain physical cues from their athletes to determine if the rewards-and-punishments system is appropriate or too harsh. While a democratic-transactional coach might not seek their athletes' opinions at a time when a quick decision is needed and instead use previous input given by the athletes to make an expedited decision. In both examples, the coaches are not compromising their core leadership beliefs regarding their role as the leader in the decision-making process or in shaping the rewards-and-punishments system, but they are both allowing for leadership flexibility so that the potential weaknesses of their chosen leadership style are mitigated.

This type of thoughtful and careful approach to leadership is in stark contrast to leadership behaviors practiced by the laissez-faire leader. However, it would be incorrect to think that laissez-faire leaders do not have a leadership plan or that they simply do not care. These common misconceptions of laissez-faire leaders have led to the leadership style often being painted in a negative light, but that assessment is not entirely fair. I say it's not entirely fair because the number of instances where a coach could be successful by solely practicing laissez-faire leadership is narrow compared to the other leadership styles discussed, but through a review of the key laissez-faire leadership behaviors, it will become apparent that, for a certain type of coach who coaches a team with a specific make up of athletes, laissez-faire leadership could be the right approach.

The plan for laissez-faire leaders begins with recruiting athletes to the team who possess the skills necessary to help make team decisions. If athletes need direct and constant supervision, they should not be part of the team since a coach who practices laissez-faire leadership is going to put a large part of the decision-making responsibility on the athletes. Coaches who are committed to laissez-faire leadership work to recruit high-performing and committed athletes, which relieves the coach from making all day-to-day team-related decisions. This approach to leadership can be viewed as delegative; however, laissez-faire leaders can be successful if they recruit the right athletes to the team who possess the knowledge, experience, and leadership abilities to take on that role.

When this leadership approach is adopted with the right group of athletes, it can lead to the athletes becoming highly motivated due to the increased opportunity each athlete has to influence team decisions and the overall direction of the team. However, that outcome is likely the result of a best-case scenario, and it is more likely that the team will experience low productivity and confusion over what the athletes' individual roles are. Laissez-faire leaders demonstrate a significant amount of trust in their athletes, which, again, is best suited for a team composed of athletes who are capable of taking on that responsibility.

A coach who practices laissez-faire leadership without the influence of any other leadership styles is probably going to have a difficult time succeeding as laissez-faire leaders generally have the lowest-performing followers. This leadership style would theoretically be best suited for professional teams composed mainly of experienced, veteran athletes who need less day-to-day guidance from their coach. Certainly, there are times within a season when a hands-off or laissez-faire approach to leadership can be beneficial for a coach; however, as the predominant leadership style practiced by a coach over a long period of time, the chances of achieving success are very limited—especially relative to the other leadership styles discussed in this chapter.

The goal of these past two chapters and having readers go through this exercise to determine their perceived and actual leadership style was twofold. First, going through this exercise demonstrates to coaches the gap or difference in the leadership style they want to practice and the style they actually practice. It also gives coaches the necessary tools and leadership knowledge to bridge that gap by changing any number of their current leadership behaviors or by adding specific behaviors to their practice. Second, this exercise gives coaches the opportunity to construct a new leadership style for themselves that they believe is best for them based on their personality, beliefs, and core leadership values. This exercise was not only intended to provide coaches with the leadership knowledge required to make great decisions, but it was also meant to inspire coaches to think more intentionally and thoughtfully about their leadership practice. A coach being intentional about their leadership practice and being committed to becoming the best leader they can be is not only essential for achieving long-term team success, it is also an integral part of building a lasting and positive team culture that inspires athletes to be leaders and to strive for improvement and greatness in all aspects of their lives.

CHAPTER VI

The previous two chapters of this book focused on bridging the gap between coaches' perceived and actual leadership styles in order to help them become more knowledgeable of and intentional about their leadership practice. The steps outlined in the previous two chapters are a guide intended to help coaches build or enhance their leadership practice through self-assessment of their current leadership behaviors and core values. However, I respect that not every coach reading this book wants to take that measured and more holistic approach to determining the best leadership style and behaviors for them to practice, and instead would prefer to use a more analytical approach to leadership as their guide. For those coaches who prefer to know what the data says before making decisions, or at least would like to be aware of what the data says, this chapter is going to give you all the data analysis you need to make your leadership choices.

In order to find out the best leadership style and behaviors for coaches to practice, I conducted research that included some of the most successful head coaches at all levels of college basketball.

Based on the data obtained in this study, I was able to determine that the most successful coaches practice transformational leadership. For reference, when I say "successful," the metric in the study used to determine if a coach was successful was based on the number of championships and post-season appearances a coach had during their career. This finding aligns with the widely excepted practical concept that one of the main jobs of a coach is to inspire and motivate their athletes, which are two of the key elements of transformational leadership.

Additionally, the data indicated that transformational leadership behaviors that focused on coaches working to develop the strengths, performance, and team commitment of their athletes were practiced most often by successful coaches. These behaviors included the use of positive language as the primary way to inspire and motivate athletes to achieve goals and improve. This is not to say that coaches should never criticize or use anything but a flowery, positive tone when conversing with their athletes, but a generally positive and uplifting message from coaches to athletes was found to be most effective. Using language such as, "We, or you, are going to get this," "Stay focused and keep trying," and, "Struggling is part of the process," were determined to be more effective communication tools for transformational leaders.

A common thread found in the transformational leadership behaviors that the successful coaches practiced most often was the word "develop." The data supports recent research in the area of athletic coach leadership that suggests the development of skills, strengths, character, performance, commitment, and other qualities is a key aspect of a coach's job. The concept of development supports the key transformational leadership element that coaches should focus on inspiring and motivating their athletes to achieve more than the athletes believe they can achieve. No one reaches their maximum potential solely by themselves. If they could, that would take a lot of the pressure off coaches to develop athletes' skills and abilities so that eventually, the athletes reach their full potential.

A coach must be willing to critically assess athletes' strengths and weaknesses and design strategies and goals to help athletes improve. Critical assessment, as a tool for helping athletes, is most effective when the findings of that assessment and path forward are explained to athletes in a respectful, positive way. It is human nature to be resistant to criticism or another person pointing out one's faults, and the wrong approach or tone can lead to athletes becoming defensive or resistant to the coach's critique of their abilities and strategies for improvement. This is where the transformational leadership approach is integral, because it focuses on positive and uplifting communication that often invokes "we" instead of "you." Saying, "These are things we can fix together," instead of, "You need to work on these things," can make all the difference in getting through to an athlete.

One aspect of leadership that can be overlooked by coaches is that it is not only their job to help athletes address their weaknesses, but also that coaches should look for ways to help athletes continue to further develop their strengths. Working to develop athletes' strengths was one of the most practiced behaviors by successful coaches, and it is very informative in explaining a key difference between successful and unsuccessful coaches. According to the data, it is not the case that unsuccessful coaches do not believe that it is their job to develop the strengths of their athletes, but rather that most of them had not considered adopting this specific behavior.

Additionally, the data indicated that unsuccessful coaches strongly perceived themselves to practice eight of the nine leadership styles tested for on the leadership survey they completed as part of my research, with autocratic leadership being the only style that successful coaches practiced more often. This finding not only indicates that successful coaches perceive themselves to more often practice autocratic leadership, but also that unsuccessful coaches perceive themselves to practice several leadership styles. This implies that a key component to help coaches achieve success is that they are more intentional about their leadership choices and have a firm idea of the leadership style they wish to practice.

When the finding that autocratic leadership was the only style practiced more often by successful coaches is viewed along with the initial finding that transformational leadership is the best style for coaches to practice, the conclusion can be drawn that practicing elements of autocratic leadership along with transformational leadership is a key factor in coaches achieving success. Another significant, differentiating factor unearthed by the data is that unsuccessful coaches more often practiced transformational leadership combined with a specific democratic leadership behavior, while successful coaches more often practiced transformational leadership combined with a specific autocratic leadership behavior. The practiced democratic leadership behavior was that coaches should seek input and the opinions of their athletes when making team decisions. The practiced autocratic leadership behavior represented the opposite belief, that coaches should be the sole decision-maker for their team.

There are several key implications from this interpretation of the data. The first is that coaches should centralize their decision-making and strive to make a majority—if not all—of the decisions for their team and athletes. Additionally, coaches should draw a clear distinction between their role as the leader of the team and their athletes' roles as the followers. Decentralizing a coaches' authority by seeking input from their athletes in order to make team decisions and treating their athletes as equals has not been shown to lead coaches to success. These findings imply that transformational leadership is the best leadership style for coaches to practice in order to achieve success when combined with the decision-making authority of autocratic leadership that draws a clear distinction between the coaches' role as the leader and the athletes' role as the followers.

In this chapter, I am not advocating that the best leadership style for all coaches is transformational leadership when combined with a specific autocratic behavior, or that coaching should immediately transform into a homogeneous profession where everyone coaches the same way. What I am advocating for in this chapter, and have been throughout this book, is that leadership practice is very personal, and that the leadership style a coach practices should align with their core leadership beliefs and values. Leadership is not an exact science, and practicing the leadership style that the data indicates is best does not ensure a 100 percent leadership success rate; however, if a coach believes in data and they are committed to using the data to drive decisions, then that approach is right. The same can be said for a coach who read this chapter and believed it was all nonsense, because that coach believes that leadership practice should derive entirely from the heart and be based on first-hand experience. To that coach: just like the coach who believes in the power of data, you are both right in your thinking, because you believe and are committed to your approach. That belief is a fundamental aspect of leadership—if a coach does not believe in their leadership approach and is unsure if it is best, then that coach will not be successful.

The goal of this book is to help coaches expand their leadership knowledge base and be able to make more intentional choices about the leadership style and behaviors they choose to practice. Whether a coach believes in data or not, it is important that coaches are exposed to different ways to view and approach leadership. This is how coaches bridge the gap between their perceived and actual leadership style and ensure that they are practicing the best leadership behaviors, whether they believe in data or not.

CHAPTER VII

What leadership style and behaviors athletes prefer and respond to best is an interesting and important question. The relationship between the leader (coach) and their followers (athletes) is influenced by the leader's specific leadership style and is directly affected by the leader's primary leadership characteristics.[34] All athletes are different, and charisma has been identified as an important leadership characteristic for coaches in order to build a promising and strong relationship with their athletes. As a team progresses through the course of a season, the relationship initially forged between the coach and the athletes will be enhanced and tested, and may grow stagnant, at different points in time. As the leader of the team, it is incumbent upon the coach to transform and modify their leadership style and behaviors based on the athletes' needs in order to continue to develop the coach-athlete relationship and foster team success.[35] An effective coach can use tenets of instructional leadership to inform their practice and be able to adjust their leadership style according to how the athletes are responding to certain leadership behaviors.[36] However, coaches must be mindful that all athletes have different learning styles, personalities, and abilities to cognitively process data and information; therefore, even leadership styles and behaviors that are successful for most athletes may not be successful for all.[37]

Facilitating learning through positive communication and instruction, conflict management, empowering learners, motivating athletes, and encouraging athletes to reach for high marks are some of the most important characteristics athletes identified they want their coach to practice. Coaches can use these characteristics and behaviors to connect with and motivate athletes socially, intellectually, and emotionally.[38] Building a strong coach–athlete relationship has been determined to be a central component of athlete development, and positive athlete development has also been found to be a key factor in team success.[39] A critical aspect of the coach–athlete relationship is dependent upon the coach giving the athletes positive feedback and providing them with social support.[40] By providing positive feedback and social support, coaches are positively reinforcing their athletes' behaviors and actions; however, the leadership style used by coaches should not be static.

Another defining aspect of coach leadership is influence. Coaches exert influence in order to direct athletes and to help them focus on individual improvement as well as the pursuit of team goals.[41] Athletic coaches, like other organizational leaders, must be encouraged to move beyond simply being managers of day-to-day responsibilities. Instead, they need to become committed to leadership.[42] By displaying strong leadership, coaches can have a positive impact on an athlete's character development, self-esteem, and social skills.[43] Furthermore, the impact of the coach as a leader is enhanced through a strong coach–athlete relationship. A strong coach–athlete relationship hinges on coaches having individualized consideration for their athletes. Individualized consideration builds trust and leads to the athletes having a greater understanding of their coach's expectations and vision for achieving success.

Coaches are responsible for developing athletes' mental, physical, and sport-specific abilities. In addition to these responsibilities, it is also the expectation for a coach's team to show significant improvement over the course of a season and win as many games or contests as possible.[44] For this reason, a coach must be more than just "a coach." Coaches are considered teachers, mentors, confidants, counselors, parental figures, and many other roles that transcend the traditional primary roles of instructor and motivator. As a result of taking on all these roles— and having the job of motivating and inspiring athletes—coaches must understand the importance of being leaders and be willing to assume that role from the beginning of their employment. Additionally, coaches must be able to identify the leadership style that best fits their character, personality, and core values, as well as the needs of their athletes, in order to achieve individual and team successes.[45]

I have always believed that it was my job as a coach to not only nurture and enhance the sport-specific abilities of my athletes and teach them the importance of working to be their best within a team concept, but also to help develop my athletes as complete people who are ready to leave college and handle the adversity that life brings. While there are many approaches that coaches take to this challenge, it has been proven time and again that athletes respond best when they are treated with respect and learn the most when they are allowed to try and fail without the looming threat of serious repercussions. This is not to say that athletes should never experience repercussions for their actions, but rather that they should be in line with the negative behavior and be clearly outlined and explained to the athletes beforehand.

Setting expectations and being consistent in upholding those expectations for all members of the team is a crucial aspect of leadership—one that athletes respect and are likely to respond to. When athletes, like anyone else, believe that they are not being treated fairly or that other members of the team are not being held to the same standard, they are unlikely to learn from the situation as they are more focused on the injustice being done to them rather than their negative behavior. Coaches need to have trust in their athletes that they will do the right things and are able to take initial directions and figure out what to do from there with minimal guidance in order to grow and be successful.

I always tell my athletes that I want them to try and fail within the team framework and rules knowing that I support them and will step in when necessary. When coaches do everything for their athletes without allowing them the opportunity to figure things out on their own and deal with adversity both big and small, it stunts the athletes' development and robs them of the opportunity to face the types of experiences that they will likely encounter throughout their lives. For example, college student-athletes are generally attuned to their scholarships, how much their bill should be, and when they are going to receive a stipend check or refund. When I was a coach, I would always get countless questions from my athletes pertaining to their scholarship, bill, or refund check, and in each circumstance I always believed that it would be more beneficial for my athletes to try and resolve the issue on their own before I jumped in, even if I could make a call and fix things right then and there. I would always point them in the right direction by telling them where to go and who to ask for, and we might even talk through how to ask their question in a respectful and clear manner, but I wanted them to try to fix the issue for themselves first.

This might seem like a small and inconsequential example, but if athletes have enough of these experiences, they will learn valuable skills such as how to interact with people they do not know, what questions are important to ask in these types of situations, and what tone will illicit the most helpful response. Like clockwork, my athletes were almost always resistant to my approach at first; however, it was always amazing to me how proud of themselves they would be when they were successful in getting something resolved without my involvement, and how self-reliant and strong they became over time. Over the course of the year, and my athletes' careers, they would almost always come to me less and less often with issues because they became so adept at solving problems themselves. Of course, if one of my athletes tried and failed, I would get involved, but I would always insist that my athletes and I worked together to solve the issue so that they could see my approach and hopefully learn from it.

Probably the word my athletes have heard me repeat over the years the most has been "we." This approach has been integral to my leadership style, because it establishes that I am on my athletes' side by always supporting them when they need it, and by showing trust in them that they will make the right decisions. However, what happens when an athlete who you have shown immense trust in violates that trust by making the wrong decisions despite your efforts, and that negative behavior reflects badly on you? The first time this happened to me in a significant way, I was very disappointed, and my failure to get through to the athlete caused me to re-evaluate my entire approach to leadership.

During my time as an assistant men's basketball coach at Chicago State, I had an athlete with whom I developed a very strong relationship. The athlete was from near the area where I grew up, and I took a fondness to him from the moment he stepped on to campus as a wide-eyed freshman. I saw that he had tremendous on-court potential and that he worked extremely hard at his craft; however, I knew right away that his lack of maturity was an issue that might derail his on-court development and pursuits. My try-and-fail-before-I-step-in-and-help approach was immediately met with resistance and an unwillingness to try, but over time, I believed that I was slowly getting through to him.

There were some bumps along the road as he progressed throughout his career, but I was determined to stay involved and not let the athlete's lack of maturity interfere with the promise he showed on the basketball court. We would have long talks in my office, and I worked hard to get through to him and help him see his faults in certain situations where he believed he was being treated unfairly. We talked often on the team bus or in the airport about how he needed to adjust certain behaviors or else he would not be able to fully earn our head coach's trust and the confidence of his teammates that he would be reliable when things got tough during the season. Finally, it all came to a head—despite my efforts, we received a report during the summer before his junior year that he was not regularly attending his summer school classes, and when he did, he was not engaged and was disrespectful.

Upon hearing this report, I immediately made excuses in my head as to why this assessment of his behavior was unfair. Before I could get any of those fake justifications out of my mouth, however, my head coach informed me that he was going to suspend the athlete and not let him play during our upcoming team trip to Costa Rica. I initially felt that this was too harsh of a punishment and would hurt the team; however, after my head coach explained that this was the right moment to take a firm stand and get the athlete's attention so that we did not let him continue down the wrong path, my perspective was changed. For a long time, I felt like I failed the athlete by not doing more to ensure that "we" did not reach this tipping point, but the more I thought about it, I realized that I had not failed the athlete—my approach had.

What I came to realize was that everything we talked about and the behaviors I had tried to change were always in pursuit of not allowing the athlete's lack of maturity to interfere with his athletic abilities and future opportunities to progress as a basketball player.

This was the wrong approach—I should have been focusing on helping the athlete see how his behaviors would interfere with his ability to be a productive member of society after he left college. I should have been trying to show him the larger picture and how his behaviors would affect his life in more profound ways, such as his ability to hold and excel at a job (in basketball or outside of it) because his employer would see him as unreliable or someone who did not work well in a team environment. During our talks, I should have been trying to illustrate to him that his actions had consequences and that those consequences were only going to get more severe and impactful on his life if he did not work to curb his negative behaviors.

Sports are a tremendous vehicle for teaching life lessons and developing an individual's character. As leaders, coaches must always have the larger picture in mind when guiding their athletes and when trying to take situations or times of adversity and turn them into teachable moments that resonate and impact their athletes. I was initially unsuccessful in helping my athlete and getting through to him because I never showed him the larger picture of how his behaviors, attitude, and actions could impact his life, and instead limited the scope of consequences to basketball.

Whether or not it is fair to ask athletic coaches to take on so much leadership responsibility is a question someone else can write a book on. Regardless of what the answers that book would reveal, coaches are being asked to take on greater leadership responsibility for their athletes seemingly every year. Additionally, coaches are often being asked to do this without the requisite leadership training and knowledge to help them be successful. It is a credit to coaches all over the world who are not only willing to accept this outsized challenge, but who take this responsibility so seriously that they are willing to seek out opportunities—such as reading this book—to develop and enhance their own leadership practice in order to best serve and mentor their athletes. Of course, if you decided to be a coach at any level of sports, it was probably in large part because you genuinely care about the development and success of the athletes you are entrusted to coach. Coaches having that deep-rooted investment in their athletes' success is what gives them a fighting chance as leaders.

CHAPTER VIII

As a leader, how should coaches define success? That is a very difficult question to answer, in large part because every coach has different values and core beliefs that drive their leadership practice and help them to set individual athlete and team goals. However, having a working and evolving definition of success is an essential element of any coach's leadership practice. Having an idea of how a coach defines success allows the coach to set standards, expectations, and goals for the individual athletes, the team, and the leader themselves. Furthermore, this definition—like leadership practice—should be evolving, constantly evaluated, and adjusted by the coach. Based on the team composition or the specific needs of individual athletes, the coach may have a fluid definition of success; however, it should always be a combination of aspirational and realistic goals and expectations. If the definition of success is too easily achieved, then it will not have the type of meaning and impact it should have after it is reached. Similarly, if the definition is too aspirational and is exceedingly difficult to achieve, then having a definition of success could become a self-defeating prophecy.

There are any number of quantifiable ways to measure success, but the tool coaches use does not necessarily have to be measured through conventional or quantifiable methods. Sometimes, a coach inherently knows whether an individual athlete or team has truly achieved success. A team that wins a great number of games might be viewed by fans as being successful based on how the fans define success for the team, but the coach might have an entirely different perspective. A coach might decide that their team has achieved success if the team wins over a certain number of games, but I would encourage coaches to broaden their definition of success beyond the traditional measures of wins and losses or post-season advancement.

A definition of success could include whether the coach believes the athletes provided maximum effort during practice and games, showed skill improvement from the beginning of the season to the end, and engaged in positive interpersonal interactions among one another and the coaches. These concepts are not necessarily quantifiable—although elements of them could be—but the larger point is that a coach has the option to include subjective elements when defining success. Early in my career as a college basketball coach, I viewed success almost exclusively through the lens of wins and losses. Over time, my definition of success evolved and became much more nuanced and inclusive of other elements that were important to my core values and what I stood for as a coach.

Wins and losses remain a part of my definition of success, and I believe they always will. considering a major goal of sports is to win and experience winning both on an individual and team level. However, providing my athletes with a great experience while they are part of the team, working to broaden their horizons through community service and volunteering, and building lasting relationships based on trust and mutual respect are now all integral elements of my personal definition of success. Within this definition of success, there are certain quantifiable goals that I want to reach, such as my team participating in a minimum number of community service and volunteer hours, or providing my athletes with a certain number of additional life skills opportunities that will hopefully help to broaden their horizons and worldview.

Even though I cannot necessarily measure the amount my emphasis on community service or acceptance has increased my athletes' willingness to give to others, or the athletes' level of acceptance for those who are different than them, there are other ways to determine whether I was successful as a leader in these areas. During my final year as an assistant coach at Chicago State, I organized a community service project right before the end of the school year for all my athletes to participate in. We had previously participated in several community service projects throughout the year, and these opportunities to give back were often met with a combination of light resistance and mild whining. Even though I had great athletes on the team that year, it can be hard sometimes for college-age kids to understand the positive impact they can have by giving back to the community or by helping those in need. Additionally, I believe that athletes are often put on a pedestal and that they can have an outsized impact through their actions because of how others see them.

I had failed to get through to some of my athletes and help them see and understand how important it was that they did things for the community and gave back. After we participated in several earlier community service projects, the feedback I received from my athletes was that they did not feel like they were making an impact or having much of an effect through their participation. This feedback immediately told me that, even though we were meeting our team goal for the number of community service projects we wanted to participate in during the year, our participation had not been successful. The athletes' participation in these projects was not successful because they were not getting what I had hoped they would out of the projects, which was a sense of shared responsibility for our community and a belief that it was important for everyone to give back and do what they can to help others who are in need.

For our last community service project of the year, we were all going to participate in a city-wide initiative where community members banded together and cleaned up their respective neighborhoods. I have always tried to instill in my athletes that we cannot expect others to support us until we show a willingness to support them, and this neighborhood clean-up was a perfect opportunity to reinforce that idea and have a positive impact in our community. Additionally, since I have always believed that I should not ask my athletes to do anything that I would not willingly do myself, I led the charge into the community and cleaned alongside my athletes and our fellow community members. We picked up trash under bridges and swept debris from alleys, we hauled trash, cleaned a community garden, and did yard work for our elderly neighbors.

When we started the day, I heard the usual whining and complaining about how it was Saturday and too cold and early to be outside cleaning. By the afternoon, a transformation occurred. The whining and complaining was replaced by laughter, camaraderie, and athletes asking me if we could stay and keep helping even after we had reached the end of our time commitment. When I spoke with my athletes afterward, the feedback was different than it had been after our other community service projects. The athletes showed a greater understanding of the impact they had that day cleaning up the community. They even asked me to commit the team to participating in the next city-wide clean-up the following fall. It took longer than I had hoped, but we finally had a successful community service experience and achieved one of the primary goals of our community service participation.

Even though that year we had not met my definition for success in terms of wins and losses, we had taken a significant step forward in how we as a team viewed community service and giving back. Of course, I want my teams to experience success in all areas, but that is not always realistic or possible. Having a definition of success that is broad and reflects a coach's personal values allows for success to be achieved in other areas aside from wins and losses. This also allows a coach and team to experience the feeling of success and achieving something significant that cannot necessarily be measured but is obvious to all who witness and participate in it. My athletes turned a corner that day and were experiencing a feeling they had not previously felt together. Those types of successes may seem small or even inconsequential to some—to me, they can be more significant and important than the successful feeling that comes after winning a game.

Being part of a team means giving a part of oneself to something that is bigger and greater than any one individual. Winning games is an amazing outcome of collective team and individual effort, but so is having other meaningful experiences as a team. These other shared experiences should be emphasized and valued by coaches so that the team can be nurtured to make each other better and learn from one another. Coaches are leaders, and they are asked to do so much more than simply design game plans and run practices. Assigning coaches so many hats to wear might not always be fair to them, but it is an opportunity for coaches to have an amazingly positive impact on their athletes in ways that without these additional roles would not necessarily be possible.

If, as a coach, you believe in the value of community service, or helping your athletes have meaningful experiences that broaden their horizons, or allowing your athletes to express their individuality as a way to teach acceptance, then you have the power and responsibility to include those values in your definition of success. As a leader, you also have the responsibility to do everything in your power to make sure that success is achieved for every team and athlete you coach. That is a tall order, and it creates a high bar for coaches to achieve in order to be successful. But, if coaches do not push themselves to do more and be more for their athletes than simply a coach who tried to win more games than they lost, then perhaps coaching is not the right profession for them.

CHAPTER IX

FINAL REFLECTIONS ON LEADERSHIP

There are many reasons why I wanted to write this book, but chief among them was that I wanted to help coaches be more intentional and thoughtful about their leadership practice. It is my hope that after reading this book, coaches will be able to more completely and confidently explain their leadership style and core leadership values to their athletes, administrators, other coaches, and anyone else who asks them about it. Coaching is an extremely difficult profession to succeed and have longevity in. I was privileged to be a college basketball coach. Even though there are leadership decisions I made and behaviors I modelled for my athletes that I would like to go back and change, ultimately, what I learned from those decisions and behaviors has shaped my current leadership practice and made me a better and more thoughtful leader.

When I reflect on my personal leadership practice, I always try to keep my core leadership values in mind so that I have proper context to assess my decisions and behaviors. I have five core leadership values that I always try to integrate into my leadership practice whenever possible. These core values have changed and evolved over time, and they all stem from key experiences I have had during my life and career. Like many young coaches, I entered the profession believing that I knew everything and was destined to be the next great coach. It was through experiences like when I committed an NCAA violation for making three athletes run for being late to open gym and having my head coach at Dartmouth put me in my place when I spoke out of turn at halftime of a game that taught me the importance of humility.

Being humble and displaying a willingness to accept advice and criticism from others are important traits for a leader to possess, but so is a leader's acceptance of responsibility for their mistakes. Had I not been willing to accept that I had made significant mistakes in both of those situations, then my growth as a leader— and as a person—would have slowed. Also, as a leader, if I am not humble enough to accept responsibility for my mistakes and take ownership of my actions and decisions, then the example I am setting for my athletes is flawed and disingenuous. When a coach is assessing problems within their team and looking for answers, the first place they should look is inward. This can be very difficult for a coach to accept and practice, but if that coach is humble and willing to accept responsibility as a leader, then that process will be much easier and beneficial.

Empathy is a leadership trait that took me a long time to learn and value as an integral part of my leadership practice. Even though I have always prided myself on developing and maintaining great personal relationships with my athletes, I did not learn the true value of having empathy for my athletes until a few years ago. At this time, I was coaching an athlete who had come to the United States for college but grew up in a country thousands of miles from Chicago. I had a good relationship with this athlete, and we talked often. During the season, I noticed that his usual vibrant and outgoing demeanor had shifted to one that was more introverted and closed-off. I was very busy and caught up in the fast pace of the season, so it was easy and convenient for me to assume the athlete's demeanor had changed because he was not getting a lot of playing time and the team was struggling.

It was not until weeks after the initial change in the athlete's behavior that I found out why. I learned from another athlete on the team that he lost a family member back home who he had not seen for several years, and he was struggling with being away and having limited contact with his family and friends. When I spoke to him about this, I rushed our conversation and failed to try to put myself in his shoes and understand what he was going through. Soon after that conversation, I felt shame for how I had failed to have empathy and understanding for what my athlete was feeling. When we talked again, I decided to relate a personal experience from my life that I hoped would help him feel better and less alone. My initial lack of empathy and understanding for what he was going through was shortsighted and undermined my belief in the importance of developing personal relationships with my athletes. From this experience, I learned the true value of empathy and the impact it can have on my athletes—both when I practice it and when I do not.

A core leadership value that I have carried with me throughout my career—and was ingrained in me from childhood—is integrity. I believe in the power of doing the right thing and modelling that for my athletes. As a leader, it is impossible to build trust within the team if there is not honesty and a strong set of guiding principles. I always try to be honest and transparent with my athletes, even when I know they do not want to hear it or it is hard for me to say. Those moments are often when a leader's words can have the greatest impact. It is my responsibility as a leader to set a standard for integrity and be willing to hold myself to that standard in front of my athletes in order to get them to believe and strive for that standard themselves. I believe in the importance of comporting oneself with dignity and that one of the truest measures of a coach is whether they are viewed by their peers and athletes as someone who always acts with integrity and tries to do things the right way. It has many times been difficult for me to sleep after tough losses or hard days where I had to make difficult decisions, but I can honestly say that I have never lost sleep wondering if I acted with integrity—that is something that I am most proud of from my time as a coach and something that I wish for all coaches.

I have been exceedingly fortunate to have had the opportunity to work at institutions all over the country and to coach athletes with different backgrounds, belief systems, and life experiences. I firmly believe that diverse and inclusive environments lead to greater understanding, acceptance, and celebration of people's individual differences and what makes them unique. It is through these shared experiences that we all have the opportunity to learn about and embrace each other's differences. However, without a leader emphasizing and embracing inclusion, these experiences and how impactful they can be is limited. One of sports' most wonderful and amazing powers is its ability to bring different people together through a common love, passion, and pursuit. As a coach and leader, it is my responsibility to promote an inclusive environment where all members of the team feel safe and accepted for who they are.

This is not always easy, as there can be times when one athlete's beliefs are in direct conflict with those of another athlete. It is through the conversations and experiences that the athletes share as team members that has the power to transcend their differences and bring those athletes and the team together. As a coach, I must work to help the athletes navigate the waters and embrace each other's differences rather than judge or criticize them. Once again, there are many potential pitfalls, but I know that if I am committed to promoting humility, empathy, integrity, inclusion, and listening, then I will have done a lot to create a positive and safe environment for my team to come together and embrace one another.

I'll be the first one to admit that I am not the best listener. It is a shortcoming of mine and something that I am constantly trying to be better at. However, the fact that I am not the world's greatest listener does not mean that listening cannot be one of my core leadership beliefs and is not just as important to my leadership practice as the other four that I am admittedly much better at practicing. An essential part of being a leader is committing oneself to finding opportunities to grow and develop specific leadership behaviors that do not come naturally. I often have a lot of thoughts racing through my head as I try to process what another person is saying to me, and this can keep me from being fully invested in listening to that person. I know that I cannot be a fully engaged and active listener if I am trying to think of a response while someone is in the middle of saying something to me. I always try to heed this advice and have tried very hard over the years to become a better listener. Through my experiences, I have learned that dedicating myself to improving my listening ability will benefit me by enhancing my other four core leadership values and help me be a better leader.

All coaches are leaders, and all leaders are different. What leadership style a coach should practice and what a coach's core leadership values are is up to that individual coach. But if coaches take the time to learn about leadership practice and make intentional decisions about the style and behaviors they choose to practice, then coaches are putting themselves in the best position to lead their team and athletes. The aforementioned leadership style and behaviors that I practice align with my core leadership values. It is my hope that, after reading this book, coaches will be better equipped to find the leadership style and behaviors that align best with their personal core leadership values in order to be the most successful and effective leaders possible.

ABOUT THE AUTHOR

After obtaining his Bachelor of Arts in history and classical studies from Indiana University, Dr. Matthew Raidbard decided to pursue his dream of being a college basketball coach. His first college basketball coaching job was at Western New Mexico University, where he also completed his Master of Arts degree in Educational Leadership. In 2018, Dr. Raidbard conducted a study on how college basketball coaches perceived themselves as leaders, finding that many coaches were unsuccessful because they lacked the necessary tools and training to be effective leaders. His findings inspired him to write this book and dedicate himself to helping coaches at all levels improve their leadership abilities so that they can be the best and most effective leaders for the athletes they are entrusted to coach.

ACKNOWLEDGMENTS

First and foremost, thank you to my parents for all their love and for always believing in me and encouraging me to pursue my dreams no matter what.

Shout out to my best friend Jeff Gottlieb for always helping me see the brighter side of things even during times when they seemed the darkest.

To Coach Tracy Dildy, thank you for taking a chance on me and teaching me one of the most important life lessons: always be loyal to those you care about.

To Dr. Crystal Laura, thank you for your unfailing optimism and belief in me as a student and person.

CITATIONS

1   Hackman, J. R., & Wageman, R. (2005). A theory of team coaching. *Academy of Management Review*, 30(2), 269-287.

2   Stornes, T., & Bru, E. (2002). Sportspersonship and perceptions of leadership: An investigation of adolescent handball players' perceptions of sportspersonship and associations with perceived leadership. *European Journal of Sport Science*, 2(6), 1-15.

3   Wells, J. E., & Aicher, T. J. (2013). Follow the leader: A relational demography, similarity attraction, and social identity theory of leadership approach of a team's performance. *Gender Issues*, 30(1-4), 1-14.

4   Kim, H. D., & Cruz, A. B. (2016). The influence of coaches' leadership styles on athletes' satisfaction and team cohesion: A meta-analytic approach. *International Journal of Sports Science & Coaching*, 11(6), 900-909.

5   Vella, S. A., Oades, L. G., & Crowe, T. P. (2012). Validation of the differentiated transformational leadership inventory as a measure of coach leadership in youth soccer. *The Sports Psychologist*, 26(1), 203-227.

6   Surujlal, J., & Dhurup, M. (2012). Athlete preference of coach's leadership style: sport management. *African Journal for Physical Health Education, Recreation and Dance*, 18(1), 111-121.

7   Acet, M., Gumusgul, O. & Isik, U. (2017). Leadership characteristics of football coaches. *Sport & Society/Sport si Societate*, 1(1), 3-9.

8   Sullivan, P. J., & Kent, A. (2003). Coaching efficacy as a predictor of leadership style in intercollegiate athletics. *Journal of Applied Sport Psychology*, 15(1), 1-11.

9   Chelladurai, P., & Saleh, S. D. (1980). Dimensions of leader behavior in sports: Development of a leadership scale. *Journal of sport psychology*, 2(1), 34-45.

10 Naidoo, P., Coopoo, Y., & Surujlal, J. (2015). Perceived leadership styles of sport administrators and the relationship with organisational effectiveness: sport management and governance. African *Journal for Physical Health Education, Recreation and Dance*, 21(Supplement 1), 167-181.

11 Chen, C. C. (2010). Leadership and teamwork paradigms: Two models for baseball coaches. *Social Behavior and Personality: an International Journal*, 38(10), 1367-1376.

12 Hersey, P. & Blanchard, K. H. (1969). Life cycle theory of leadership. *Training and development Journal*, 23(5), 26–34.

13 Hersey, P. (1984). *The situational leader.* New York City, NY: Warner Books.

14 Bass, B. M. (1997). Does the transactional-transformational leadership paradigm transcend organizational and national boundaries? *American psychologist*, 52(2), 130-139.

15 Vella, S. A., Oades, L. G., & Crowe, T. P. (2010). The application of coach leadership models to coaching practice: Current state and future directions. *International Journal of Sports Science & Coaching*, 5(3), 425-434.

16 Bass, B. M., Waldman, D. A., Avolio, B. J., & Bebb, M. (1987). Transformational leadership and the falling dominoes effect. *Group & Organization Studies*, 12(1), 73-87.

17 Stenling, A., & Tafvelin, S. (2014). Transformational leadership and well-being in sports: The mediating role of need satisfaction. *Journal of applied sport psychology*, 26(2), 182-196.

18 Schruijer, S. G., & Vansina, L. S. (2002). Leader, leadership and leading: From individual characteristics to relating in context. *Journal of Organizational Behavior*, 23(7), 869-874.

19 Bass, B. M., Waldman, D. A., Avolio, B. J., & Bebb, M. (1987). Transformational leadership and the falling dominoes effect, 73-87.

20 Vella, S. A., Oades, L. G., & Crowe, T. P. (2012). Validation of the differentiated transformational leadership inventory, 203-227.

21 Chelladurai, P., & Saleh, S. D. (1980). Dimensions of leader behavior in sports, 34-45.

22 Chase, M. A. (2010). Should coaches believe in innate ability? The importance of leadership mindset. *Quest, 62*(3), 296-307.

23 Pratt, S. R., & Eitzen, D. S. (1989). Contrasting leadership styles and organizational effectiveness: The case of athletic teams. *Social Science Quarterly, 70*(2), 311-322.

24 Cote, J., & Gilbert, W. (2009). An integrative definition of coaching effectiveness and expertise. *International Journal of Sports Science & Coaching, 4*(3), 307-323.

25 Bass, B. M., & Avolio, B. J. (1994). *Improving organizational effectiveness through transformational Leadership.* New York, NY: Sage Publishing.

26 Pratt, S. R., & Eitzen, D. S. (1989). Contrasting leadership styles and organizational effectiveness, 311-322.

27 Burns, J. (1978). *Leadership.* New York, NY: Harper and Row Publishers.

28 Bass, B. M. (1985). *Leadership and performance beyond expectations.* New York, NY: Collier Macmillan.

29 Burns, J. (1978). *Leadership.* New York, NY: Harper and Row Publishers.

30 Bass, B. M. (1985). *Leadership and performance beyond expectations.*

31 Lewin, K., Lippitt, R., & White, R. (1939). Patterns of aggressive behavior in "experimentally created" social climates," *Journal of Social Psychology, 10*(1), 271-299.

32 Lewin, K., Lippitt, R., & White, R. (1939). Patterns of aggressive behavior, 271-299.

33 Lewin, K., Lippitt, R., & White, R. (1939). Patterns of aggressive behavior, 271-299.

34 Schruijer, S. G., & Vansina, L. S. (2002). Leader, leadership and leading, 869-874.

35 Turman, P. D. (2001). Situational coaching styles: The impact of success and athlete maturity level on coaches' leadership styles over time. *Small Group Research, 32*(5), 576-594.

36 Neumerski, C. M. (2013). Rethinking instructional leadership, a review: What do we know about principal, teacher, and coach instructional leadership, and where should we go from here?. *Educational administration quarterly, 49*(2), 310-347.

37 Stevens-Smith, D., & Cadorette, D. (2012). Coaches, athletes, and dominance profiles in sport: addressing the learning styles of athletes to improve performance. *Physical Educator, 69*(4), 360-374.

38 Noland, A., & Richards, K. (2014). The relationship among transformational teaching and student motivation and learning. *The Journal of Effective Teaching, 14*(3), 5-20.

39 Vella, S. A., Oades, L. G., & Crowe, T. P. (2012). Validation of the differentiated transformational leadership inventory, 203-227.

40 Chelladurai, P., & Saleh, S. D. (1980). Dimensions of leader behavior in sports, 34-45.

41 Chase, M. A. (2010). Should coaches believe in innate ability?, 296-307.

42 Pratt, S. R., & Eitzen, D. S. (1989). Contrasting leadership styles and organizational effectiveness, 311-322.

43 Cote, J., & Gilbert, W. (2009). An integrative definition of coaching effectiveness and expertise, 307-323.

44 Becker, A. J. (2009). It's not what they do, it's how they do it: Athlete experiences of great coaching. *International Journal of Sports Science & Coaching, 4*(1), 93-119.

45 Vella, S. A., Oades, L. G., & Crowe, T. P. (2012). Validation of the differentiated transformational leadership inventory, 203-227.